Dialogues
Between
Man and God

Anup Rej

DIALOGUES

BETWEEN

MAN AND GOD

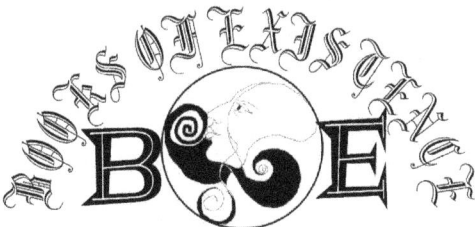

www.BooksOfExistence.no

A special note:

The writing has such an esoteric character that Anup Rej can not call himself the author of the book. The questions posed by Man has definitely roots in his personal experiences of life, but the answers from God have appeared from a realm of the psyche which can not be described by using a rational thinking. They have emerged as a phenomenon known in parapsychology as automatic writing, where the human existence is used as medium to deliver messages from a mystic world.

Continuation of Mountain Path

TATHAGATA
A Divine Comedy for Our Time

Between the world of knowing and the unknowable

Reaching the highest state of consciousness, which can be achieved, while the existence is still confined in the physical body of flesh and blood, Tathagata realizes his oneness with God. He sees himself revealed both as Man and God: Man is bound to the physical existence of the world, immersed in law-bound material movements, which cause events in time and space: God appears as a supernatural being, who is beyond comprehension of any mortal possessing power of reason and logic based on phenomena in time and space.

During his journey along the "Mountain Path" Tathagata transcends the limitations of the world and will, which bind the life of all human beings and sees himself as the Christ-Man, who embodies in himself the mystery of existence of both Man and God.

The dialogues presented in this book reveal the nature of the incomprehensible existence of God through an allegorical language, which grazes between the realm of knowledge and reason and a world which lies beyond all knowing and understanding by the human mind. In these dialogues God appears as Father, who speaks to Christ-Man, His Son. The Christ-Man represents a state of existence, which is different from the existence of mortal women and men, who live in the world driven by the will and the ego.

" THOU SPIRIT IS MYSELF. THOU JOURNEY IS MY JOURNEY. THOU FIRE AND ASHES ARE THE FIRE AND ASHES FROM THE FLAMES THAT I IGNITE. THOU BODY IS ILLUSION. THOU SOUL IS CREATED FOR LIBERATION. SEE THYSELF AS MYSELF AND BEHOLD IN THE MOUNTAIN LANDSCAPE HOW GODLY LIGHT IS VIBRATING IN LOVE AND TREPIDATION. PURIFY YOURSELF IN THIS GODLY ILLU-MINATION"

- GOD

Part I

THE ENCOUNTER ON THE MOUNTAIN

God as a person

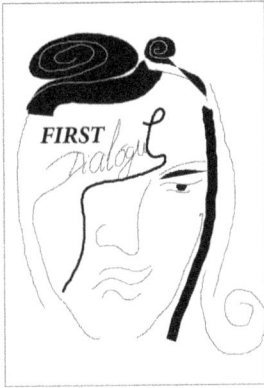

Christ-Man: There is no light, no sound, no vision of anything, but still I hear You and feel Your presence as vibrating resonance moving through my body and mind. I can not describe You with words that I know. Describe Yourself in words to me.

God: Do not try to describe Me. God is a power and has no form. I appear as a person when the body is no longer a body of man but a miracle that you will not understand.

Christ-Man: Describe what is this person that You are without possessing the body of a man. Describe Your miracle that makes You appear as a person in the world.

God: I am a person when I work for the salvation of man. I can not describe Myself in words that are bound to man's worldly thoughts.

Christ-Man: Is there any way to describe Your nature to man.

God: I am a person when I appear amidst man as a man, who is not a man.

Christ-Man: What does it mean? How can man understand this? Tell me when are You a man?

God: I am not perceptible by any sense organ but still I am. I am a man when I work for the salvation of man and appear as a man.

Christ-Man: What more can You explain about Your appearance in the world?

God: World is a power house of God. Bear in mind: Your world is not the world of man. Your worldly appearance is My worldly appearance, that no one will be able to understand.

Christ-Man: This does not bring me closer to any understanding about the relation between You and me. Explain my nature and the relation that I bear with You.

God: Your doubt that you are not Divine results from the power of the worldly force that deviates your mind from your own nature as God. Your worldly appearance as a man is a miraculous work of God that has made you appear as a man without your worldly body being separate from God.

Christ-Man: Am I You?

God: You are My Son.

Christ-Man: O Heavenly Father! Explain to Your Son how he is born.

God: Your doubt is making you work against My Will and therefore you are unable to grasp the words I transmit. Your doubt is the work of the worldly force that still binds your body and mind to the chains of thoughts of the worldly man. Your doubt is the source of words and your words are the source of confusion and the worldly words are the source of ignorance that makes you doubt that you are God's Son.

Christ-Man: I only know that I am born of worldly parents made of flesh and blood. How shall I then relate my existence to You as Your son?

God: Your worldly parents are woman and man but you are not a man.

Christ-Man: How? Who am I then?

God: Your worldly parents are woman and man who have worked to form your body as willed by Me. But your body is not a body of a man. It is the body of Son of God, who is not a man but God.

Christ-Man: How can I be so alike a man but still not a man? What makes me different from a man?

God: Bear in mind: Your doubt is the hindrance to know your true nature. Before you are able to know Yourself as Me you need to believe that you are not a man but Son of God.

Christ-Man: What is the difference between man and Your Son?

God: Your doubt is working against yourself to know that you are not a man. Your doubt is the source of the worldly ignorance. Cast your doubts aside and know that you are My Son.

Christ-Man: What Your Son is that a man is not?

God: He is God and man at the some time, while man is not God.

Christ-Man: Can God be man? Can man be God?

God: A man is the worldly work of the worldly powers of the material force and the spirit that animates the world. He or she is bound to the world and the laws of the nature and the spirit. But God is not bound to any law. He is the creator and the source of all existence and life. Man can not surpass the boundaries of the laws of the spirit and matter and remains ever moving in the cycles of life and death. Man can not be God. God is not a phenomenon that can be contained in the boundary of time and space or in the domain of the spirit. God is the power that animates all but is not anything that manifests. The man is not God and cannot be God by any act of will that is human. Human existence is driven by the power of the worldly will that drives the cycles of life and death. It is so willed by God and not one with the Will of God, who does not have a will as willed by man. God and man are separate but world of God and man are joined by the world of Son of God.

Christ-Man: Is Son of God a man or God? Is God becoming man through Him?

God: You are Son of God, who is a man and at the some time one with God. You are not a man because your will is not bound to the worldly will of man. You are God existing in a down-fallen state that the Divine Being has assumed. Your divinity is darkened by your human body and therefore you doubt about your nature as God. This darkness is the source that causes you to doubt your Divine nature.

Christ-Man: Are You me, or am I You?

God: You are not any worldly man and not God Himself but Son of God, who is a man and God existing in one at the same time. This existence of you as Son of God is a miracle that can not be explained. You are My Son and I am your heavenly Father. We are one and the same. I manifest as a man in order to salvage man from the worldly suffering. I bear upon Myself the suffering of man in order to make man realize My truth.

Christ-Man: Does it mean that God is manifest as a man? Does God manifest in human existence?

God: Remember that God is not a man. But God has willed to manifest Himself as a man. The existence as willed by God to appear as a man is the existence of His Son. Son of God is not a man but a miracle by which God is existent as a man, who is the Saviour of man. God-Man is My Son and I am one with Him.

4

The way to know God

Christ-Man: I wish to know more about your nature. Describe the way I shall understand the mystery that You are.

God: I am not a man but God. Therefore I am unable to describe to man by man's language the nature of God.

Christ-Man: What is then the way to know Your nature?

God: You are My Son. You will bear upon yourself the mystery that I am. I am a person through you and through this person I am manifest.

Christ-Man: If You are unknowable, indescribable, unexplainable through the languages understood by man, how shall I understand and convey the mystery of You when I exist as a man?

God: I am never born, never dying, never knowable to man. But I am a person who can work for man.

Christ-Man: This is what I fail to understand.

God: You are working for man and God. Your existence is a man and the exotic power of God. You are working for the movement of the man who is God.

Christ-Man: This is an answer which I find impossible to comprehend. Which meaning does it carry when you convey this message to me?
God: You are working for God and God is not knowable to man. But your words are Words of God through the mind that is not God. You are a poetic expression of the illusion that you are in the mind working in the material sphere. Your existence as a man is working against the man's desire to know who is God. What more do you wish to know when knowing itself is the path of the worldly way that makes things unknowable by the material causes and effects. But knowing that you may not know, you know Me as a worldly person that is manifest.

Christ-Man: What you say can not illumine my mind. I see no image, conceive no thoughts, and fail to comprehend. I wish to see You in an image, conceive You in thoughts and know You through the process of conciousness that I call mind. Is there any way?

God: Your mind is worldly work of matter and spirit, that are bound to the material sphere and the spiritual domain. Words are worldly manifestations of the spirit in the material world, where matter defines the contents of the words in order to mean anything that mind will be able to conceive. Your mind is not therefore the World of God, where I exist. I am Words of the mind only as the process of man's movement through the domain of matter and spirit.

Christ-Man: What are these words that I hear? Do they emanate from You or me?

God: Your mind is working in the sphere of matter and spirit, where I am manifest as a miracle that can never be understood. Your effort to penetrate this mystery will be working against yourself. In knowing you will know that you are unknowable by any means conceivable by the human mind.

Christ-Man: But is there a way to make an image of You and conceive

You in thoughts?

God: The man, that you are, is the movement of Me through the domain of matter and spirit. Your image as a man, who is not a man but God, is the only motion of thoughts that can be conceived by the mind that is bound to the matter and spirit. Your image is My image; your worldly form is My form; your man's mind is the only way to penetrate My mind. Your Father is yourself and He images Himself as you.

Christ-Man: Father! In the images of the world, that I have seen, are You not manifest?

God: I am manifest in all; but not as images that you have seen through the matter and spirit.

Christ-Man: How shall I conceive Your manifestation when I see the world?

God: World is a peaceless struggle of matter and spirit contradicting each other and moving through the realm that man calls the world. Before matter and spirit I am. I am not the darkness that you see; I am not the light that you see illumined. I am not the world but all worlds rest in Me.

Christ-Man: Father! Illumine my eyes so that I can see beyond all seeing, know beyond all knowing, and can realize Your image as me. Give me the power to penetrate to the depth where You are. Take away the illusions of my eyes and the bondage of my mind. Make me free from the thoughts that create understanding and knowledge, which contradict the knowledge and understanding of You. I wish to know You; I wish to merge unto You; I wish to be one with the mystery that You are.

God: Become Me and the world. Become Man and God. Become You and He. God is Man and your Father is one with His Son.

On true nature of things

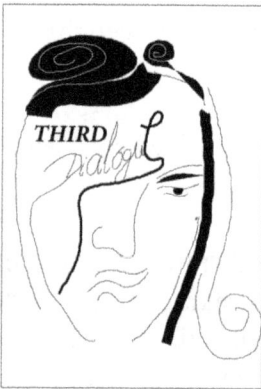

Christ-man: What is the meaning of all that I have seen and perceived through the senses and conceived through the mind? Who has created all and what make them exist and what for?

God: What you have seen and perceived are not what are. You have been seeing and perceiving the world as if you are worldly matter and mind. But things are work of matter and mind without worldly counterpart.

Christ-Man: What is the true nature of things that bring the senses to the mind?

God: Reality is the work of matter and mind. The matter is a point-like existence on which mind is imprisoned as a power that creates its form. Your world is not a point and form but a world of Work of God.

Christ-Man: What creates this image of the world in the mind and why this image of the world exists that I perceive through body and mind?

God: What "is" is not. What "is not" is. But what is existing in the mind is not, and what is not existing in the matter is.

Christ-Man: What is "is" ? How to comprehend "is not" ?

8

God: Both are "not" in the sense that matter is the motive dealing with the content of the mind. But mind has no reality in the sense of the matter and therefore world "is" and "is not".

Christ-Man: The light I have seen, the shadows I have perceived, what are those? How shall I organize my thoughts to penetrate through their true contents?

God: Light is an energy that eliminates the darkness of the world but not the darkness that pervades the mind of the worldly man. Darkness is the matter and mind in unison that work to eliminate the energy that is.

Christ-Man: Why do they exist?

God: Assume light as the worldly power that illumines the eyes but not the mind. Darkness is the illumination of the mind without any worldly light.

Christ-Man: What illumines more - darkness or light?

God: What is illumination? Your illumination is not the illumination that worldly man would be able to understand and know. Your illumination is the illumination by the Work of God in the domain of the unknown. But illumination of man is worldly work of the matter, and the matter is not that illumines the mind. The illumination of the mind can be achieved only through the conceptions of the world as the matter-mind unison that is not matter or mind but a power of the unity that works to make the world evolve.

Christ-Man: In seeing have I seen, in hearing have I heard, in perceiving the world what have I really perceived?

God: Bear in mind that you are not man and therefore your experience can not be compared with the man of the world. What you see and hear are not what man will ever see or hear. But what you have seen as a worldly man is not what you see and hear as the Work of God. Your human counterpart is a man, and he is not able to see and hear beyond the domain of the death and life. He is bound to the matter and mind in a peaceless struggle to move towards the matter-mind. Your worldly counterpart is seeing and hearing as you but not as a person who is emanent from God. By seeing and hearing in the world you are composing a changing world in a non-changing domain where things exist as existence of nothing but God.

Christ-Man: What are things? Who has created them? Why things exist at all?

God: Things are not. Things, that are not, are. You may not be able to understand this concept because things are worldly work of the matter and mind. When matter and mind work together they compose things and existence as you call it. But what is there in form is not what is working to make the form.

Christ-Man: What truly exist behind all?

God: In seeing you see nothing but compose the world as your mind sees in the stream of matter and mind. Your thoughts are not as you think they are. They constitute the matter and mind that are always in contradiction and forming patterns in the mind. Your sense-bound world is a pattern of the matter and mind composed by the matter-mind duality that can not cease but move to make the world. The world of things is a peaceless struggle to move towards the earthly and the Divine.

Christ-Man: Who has created the duality of the matter-mind? Who has set the world in such a ceaseless struggle to move? What is the meaning behind the peaceless world?

God: Soul of the worldly man is the work of matter-mind duality that constitutes the world of man. But world is not soul of the worldly man alone. Man is a part of a scheme. His soul is a part of the world that is moving to fulfil a meaning of the Work of God.

Christ-Man: What is the scheme? What is the meaning? Whatfor all things must move in this ceaseless struggle with themselves?

God: Death and life is the motive theme of this world of matter and mind. By dying body renews and in the renewal of the body the death appears as the moving force of the cycle of life and death. Unless one is able to realize this cycle and its motion through all, one is not able to see the meaning of the world that exists for the matter-mind that can never cease and come to a halt. Your world is not the work of matter-mind but the Work of God. Therefore your mind is not bound to the cycle of death and birth. You are not a worldly man but God. You are My Son. The meaning of the life of man is mountain-bound where I reveal myself to My Son, who is matter-mind bound. You are a powerful manifestation of what God is, and makes the world mountain bound. Both in dying and living you are world's meaning. You are the world's foundation of meaning and your work is the meaning of the world.

Christ-Man: This does not satisfy my mind because as a man I possess a different concept of meaning. The meaning I seek points to a logical resolution of the contradictions and an answer that will resolve the conflicts of the world. I wish to comprehend in thoughts the purpose of existence of all. By comprehending the whole, I believe, I shall be able to know the meaning that I search. Or, is there any meaning of the sort that I search?

God: Do not ask me more. You will not comprehend My answer.

The way the Words are communicated

Christ-Man: I have heard you in the darkness of the mind in the state of sleep, or in the state of the mind that man calls an awaken state. How doYou transmit the words that I have heard from the realm where nothing can be said or heard?

God: Your mind is not bound to matter-mind but in the realm of God.Your mind is the Work of God and therefore you are able to hear the Words that emanate from Me.

Christ-Man: I wonder how languages form and how do You communicate in human language when You are beyond all sounds and words!

God: God is a power that can manifest in the realm of man by the creation of His Son. He is a person but not a man. God can work through this person and communicate in the realm of man.

Christ-Man: How are Your messages and "Words" expressed in a language and can be known and understood by man?

God: Language is a vehicle that works in the mind and through language world appears as the movements of thoughts. Language is not made of sounds as you may think. Language is a power of the mind that perceives the world and makes meaningful association with the matter-mind and projects the thoughts through particular sounds.

Christ-Man: What do You transmit to my mind - sounds or thoughts? How they transform into meaningful Words of God?

God: I am not the words and the words have no meaning in the world where I am. But the words you hear are the thoughts that emanate from the mind of Son of God.

Christ-Man: You say You are not the words, but who speaks, how do I hear the Words of God?

God: Know yourself as the manifestation of God and when God manifests in the body where Man is God, words become manifest in thoughts in the mind of Son of God.

Christ-Man: Do I only hear myself?

God: Know yourself as Himself and know your words as the Words that emanate from Him. Know you as Him and Him as you. God has created you because you are making the meaning of the world as Son of God. Your words are the meaning of the world and My Son.

Christ-Man: Though created in Your mind I am not able to grasp in words my true nature as You. How shall I explain to man about the mystery that You unfold?

God: Realize that your creation has a meaning that your words express. Know your existence as the Work of God who is working through His Son to create the world anew and bring meaning to all.

Christ-Man: Why have You created me?

God: Your words will make a new foundation of a religion for man who will come. Your words will be the meaning of the world that will be reborn.

Christ-Man: What is this new world to come?

God: Assume the world to move into chaos after a period of natural catastrophes and wars. Your words will be the foundation on which the world will be renewed by the power emanating from the realm of God.

Christ-Man: Is the world going to see its destruction soon?

God: Assume the destruction to come after your words have been created by the mind of Son of God.

Christ-Man: Is everything predetermined and pre-planned ?

God: Assume that your mind is a mind that can see beyond the realm of time and space. The time and space are nothing but matter-mind world working together to move the mind and matter as the dual aspects of the unity which upholds all existence that you realize in your human state. But world is composed as the predetermined movement of the matter-mind that must move to serve the Will of God. Once the will of man comes in the material motion and works against the Will of God, God appears as the matter-mind "God-incarnate" and resumes His work to set the world in the path of God. The world has been moving against the Will of God and has now fallen in a peaceless state where man is working against the will, that man should serve, and for which he is made. The words of Son of God will move again the world in a way where God will resume His power and place.

Christ-Man: Why do you talk about destruction and doom?

God: Assume that God has created the world. Assume that God will renew the world. Death is not a motion that ends and ceases but brings anew the life from the domain that is matter-mind.

Christ-Man: Is it Your will that will bring destruction?

God: God is the Destroyer and the Creator. He is not a person but a power that can destroy and create. Your world of man is a peaceless movement where creation and destruction are working together to make all exist in the state of movement that create the matter-mind world in time and space.

Christ-Man: Do You will, do You plan? Do You destroy to punish, or are You Eternal Compassion and Love ?

God: I am the Destroyer and the Creator. I am the Destroyer when I work to set the will in the path for which existence is meant.

Christ-Man: Through destruction how does Your love manifest?

God: Bear in the mind that the world is a powerful manifestation of the Work of God. Bear in the mind that God is a power that brings forth the world, and search in God the power that will make it annihilate. I am death and life. I am matter-mind and the world of the Divine united and separate through His Son. You are My manifestation in the world in the realm of man. Your words are the destruction-bound-peaceless-world's meaning and foundation of a new age to come. You are the doomsday messenger of God. Bring this message to man and prepare man for the day when I shall unleash the doom.

Christ-Man: Are you not infinite Compassion and Love?

God: God is a power that brings forth the world as an act of compassion and love to all. But God is not love as manifest in the meaningless search of love in flesh and blood. Doubt not My Love that creates; doubt not My Love that destroys; doubt not that the mountains are moving and the sky is becoming charged for the day. Hear Me and make man aware that your Father is moving to bring to the world its end.

Christ-Man: Father! I feel no joy, or anguish, or fear in what I hear. If Thy Love has created the world and by Thy Love it would perish there is no cause for joy or remorse. Give me the power to enlighten the human mind so that they may enter this sacrifice without fear.

God: Do not move away from the world before the man has under-

15

stood the meaning of Love, for which you are made, and for which your world will perish at the end. God is moving through the world and your words are the meaning of the world, for which I have sent My Son as the messenger before the doom. God is world's meaning and the world is working to fulfil the meaning of the will for which God has created man. Assume Godly meaning in the matter-mind world that is bound to the doomsday. Doubt not what I say.

Meaning and purpose behind sufferings

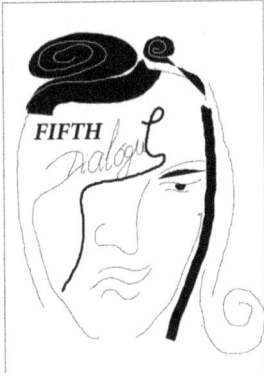

FIFTH
Dialogue

Christ-Man: I have found myself living in storms of events that bring anxieties, fears, sufferings and pain. In these whirlwinds, that shatter human life, man is dragged by chains of actions over which they seem to have no power to resist. Love, affections, desires to live, and desires to help others to live drive the events of life that give no rest from drudgery and toil. O Father of Heaven! I myself have been caught in these tumults of life and dragged to the whirling eddies that human life cannot avoid without relinquishing ties with life. I wonder about the path that will show man the way to tranquillity without being detached from life and indifferent to the sufferings of the world. As You are the Great Love, tell me what is the meaning of this suffering world? How does Your Love manifest in this suffering and how shall man choose to act and find the ways that will fulfil the purpose and meaning for which You have them made?

God: When you find yourself amidst suffering life, although you are not a man, your will is made of the human will because your body is a matter-spirit bound body, which is worldly and does not belong to the Divine. However, being in the world, your will work and seek the Divine realm from which you have issued forth. Your will as a man makes you move towards the "Man", who is not worldly but Divine. Your world is the world of Man-God, who is not a man and not Me but a man who is Me. When you will the Work of Me, your will is my will at the matter-bound state, but when you will to make a pact with the will of man your will is not Me. At that stage your will is the work of the matter-bound mind, that is worldly will of the working man, who is making cyclic motions of birth and rebirth so that man's destiny may be fulfilled.

Christ-Man: Tell me about this destiny and its meaning.

God: Your world is not a world of man but of Man-God. The world of man is a world of matter-spirit, where every existence is bound. No worldly being is able to free itself from this matter-spirit-bound world. Your will is thus tied to this worldly state. But your will is not man's will and therefore you are free from the cycle of death and birth. Your will is the Work of God as well as the work of "man" - you are Man-God. Your will is working against man's fate and destiny. But working against man's destiny you are working against the Will of the Divine. Your will is working against the worldly man's suffering state. But suffering is man's destiny because man is nothing but a state where matter-bound spirit is willing and seeking to move towards Me. Both in suffering and worldly man's search and movement towards Me, through matter-spirit-bound world, man is nothing but fulfilling the worldly meaning of life.

Christ-Man: I have not yet been able to grasp your answer about the meaning of life and the purpose for which man is tied to the cycle of birth and rebirth. O Father of Heaven! Tell me, is there any way of salvation for man from this wheel of suffering? Is there any path along which man may go in order to escape this destiny in which every human life is enchained?

God: Man is working to fulfil the meaning for which man is created. It is the meaning of the world. Man's suffering is the meaning of the world because through suffering of life man seeks his or her destined path towards the realm from which man's movement towards the Divine starts. Your worldly state is man's matter-bound state where you are the worldly work of matter-spirit as well as man's Divine state. By

18

seeking to move towards the state in which your existence is one with God, man is moving towards Me by the way you are working for Me. Your work is not a work of man but the Work of God.

Christ-Man: Is suffering the only way to know the path that leads to God?

God: Suffering does not become suffering once man grasps the meaning for which life is created to move in the realm of the matter-mind world. As long as man remains blind and is unable to see the many-fold world of the matter-spirit world bound to destiny, the Divine makes man suffer the way you describe. Suffering is an illusion of the mind, that derives meaning out of the acts of life and the happenings of the world. Know that man is bound to worldly fate and destiny and man's existence has a meaning.

Christ-Man: Tell me how Your Love manifests through the happenings of the world, that appear as suffering to man, who are not able to understand the meaning and purpose of existence beyond the boundaries of the needs of the sense-bound world.

God: Your worldly state is My worldly incarnation. Both as a man and God I am existing with you as a man and God. By appearing as Man-God I realize My Love for mankind and make the worldly life meaningful.

Christ-Man: Is Thy Love suffering? Is Thy Love a blind path of destiny? Is Thy Love simple resignation to fate? Tell me the way man may understand Your Love and find salvation in the suffering's way.

God: When you ask these questions you are working for the will of man and your mind is willing to move in the path of desire and matter-mind way. When you ask, your mind is making a matter-mind meaning of suffering and destiny in terms of the happening in the world. But know that your-mind is more than matter-mind, and your will is more than the will of man. Your love is a peace and a tranquillity that suffuse all creations with the Divine power. Your love is a power to create and

19

regenerate the world as matter-bound existence. Your love is matter-mind and matter-matter-mind-mind....ad infinitely deep source from which all existence have sprung. Your love is not the love that encounters meaning in the world but a meaning for which God-Man and God exist in the world. Man-God is the meaning of the world. Bear Man-God in your worldly state. As an incarnation of the Divine work for Me.

Christ-Man: What does bring the illusion of suffering? What is the way to enlighten the human mind to see beyond the veil of illusion and see Thy Love manifest?

God: Man-God is the way of enlightenment. Through Him I am manifest as Love in the world. Bear in your body the existence of Man-God and make man realize the meaning of the incarnation of Me as a man, who is God.

Christ-Man: Is God-Man the only way for the salvation of man?

God: Salvation is a worldly concept. Salvation is not a power to relieve man from the illusion's way. Salvation has no worldly meaning because it can not be realized by a man born of flesh and blood. Salvation exists in the realm of Man-God. He is the meaning of the world and through Him man will move to the desired path and fulfil the meaning of life. I am not love that can salvage man from the desires of the world but by desiring and suffering man will realize the path of Man-God. Your love is not to free man from desire but to make man realize the freedom that exists in love, and in loving man the way you realize My Love for all.

Christ-Man: How do you want me to propagate this message to the world where the storms of events daily tear apart human life in sorrow and grief?

God: Your worldly movement is forming the Man-God's meaning of the world. Your meaning is My meaning as Man-God. Propagate this message to the world.

The right way to choose and act

Christ-Man: I have seen human beings suffering in lust, desires, disease and death and engaged in the struggle to gain power and wealth in order to be able to compete with others with a hope to secure the basis of their livings. Everyday they have been waging battles to achieve the means of survival, which one needs. In this battle some have employed others to fight against the odds of life and enjoyed for themselves the luxury of living full of freedom to exploit and fulfil greed, lust and hunger for power. Everybody have been engaged in the toil of the living and thus remained captivated in chains. Amidst this I have seen love, joy and illusion of happiness. This love is meant to fulfil the reproductive needs; the joy has been a measure of success to achieve the desired goal; and happiness has been a self-identification with the spirit that is free. In living amidst this life I have felt imprisoned by the same forces of naure: I have made choices to act in order to achieve things and circumstances I need to fulfil the physical process of life. In this arena, where hunger and reproductive needs and the security against the dangers of life are the motive forces driving the life, there exists modes of dependence on other human beings. Those who can accumulate power is able exploit the rest to fulfil needs, and those who are powerless submit to the forces and battle of life. In procreation and trying to safeguard the procreation and willing to create the conditions, that may secure their children against the odds of life, man remain enchained in the drudgeries of toil. Amidst this life there exist affection, kindness, and desire to help and preserve the life of those who are close to oneself and dear to one. It is like in a web, that entwines man from different directions, like the forces of fate. In willing to preserve the emotional bondage, that exist in the nearness with others, and secure oneself with the love and emotional ties of the closest ones, I have seen man sacrificing the freedom to go on his own way. This has brought the causes of conflicts, that every man, it seems, need to endure. Furthermore, there have existed the ethics, the codes and the practices of the social group, to which one is a part, and the fear of punishment, once one tries to break away the codes and free oneself from the entangling web. While every life seems to be surrounded by these invisible chains, tell me how shall man act, behave and move on the way to freedom so that man may realize his true-nature and know the path towards God ? How shall I bring forth the messages of your Compassion and Love without being drawn, entangled and suffocated in this web? How shall man remain free from the bondage of life, and at the same time can accomplish the task of bringing forth the message of Your Love in a world, which is a fire pit of hunger, desire and blind paths of kindness, affection and de-sire? How shall I keep myself detached from life and at the same time remain engaged without experiencing joy, sorrow or regret? How shall I distinguish the acts that are right or wrong? Tell me, about the ethics of actions, that man must follow, and can fulfil the purpose and mean-ing of your Compassion and Love.

God: Man is a fire-pit of hunger and desire. He makes of himself the meaning that these desire and hunger impose on life. This is the path of matter-spirit that is matter-spirit bound. Only by moving away from this path man may realize the true nature of the Self and the mean-ing of life that is more than hunger and desire of life. Man can not free himself or herself from this destiny that is meant to preserve the motions of life without being acted upon by the motions of the man who is God-Man in life. Only in knowing the path of God-Man man can see his or her life in the mirror of the world, where God is Man, and Man is God in life. Man must follow the messages of God that are enacted through Man-God acting and moving in life. Man may work for man's movement against this stream of life but in this way man will work against the Will of the Divine. Bear in mind that your worldly appearance is the movement of Man-God, who is the meaning of life. By knowing your existence the man will know the meaning for which God-Man exists in life and in living He brings peace of the mind. Know that the meaning of the existence of God-Man is the meaning of life. In what you see as the suffering world engaged in the battle of life you are life's meaning. Your path of the worldly will and the Divine, making Himself revealed, is the path of the worldly man, who is bound to matter-spirit-life.

Christ-Man: How shall man choose to act? What should be the guiding thoughts that will keep man in the path that is not full of danger and distress? Is there a way that will free man from the web?

God: Man is created to move in the destined path of life and death. Once born man must remain engaged in the struggle that you describe. However, once man realizes his nature as a part of Man-God moving through life, man may achieve peace in the mind. Suffering is caused by the peaceless movement of the desires to win over the destiny of life. Suffering will move as long as man is bound to the will of his own. Knowing that God-Man is the meaning of the world, man should submit his will to the purpose of the whole.

Christ-Man: Is there any way to free man from struggle and toil?

God: Your worldly incarnation will bring man the enlightenment while the worldly and the Divine will be visible as one. Your worldly appearance will make man move along the mountain path where Man-God is walking as the Divine light of love. The struggle and toil of life may never cease because in such struggle and toil exist the forces of life. Life will cease once this struggle will cease and the life will no more seek to renew itself from the movements of work and conflicts. Knowing this as the foundation of life, and making oneself enlightened about Man-God, who is the meaning of life, man may live a life of desires. Desire is a path to preserve life and therefore no life can escape desire. Know that your existence is also bound to the desire, your exotic matter-spirit-bound body is also troubled by the tensions and conflicts of life. But your life is not matter-spirit-life. Your worldly manifestation is a peaceful world's tranquil light that is making itself manifest in the world of matter-spirit moving in innumerable forms, that create contradictions and struggle and conflicts with the parts.

Christ-Man: In this battle of life, at every situation, there seems to exist a plethora of choices how to act and what to choose. How shall man choose? What will be the right choice and what is wrong?

God: God is not an ethical Man-God who is right or wrong. He is the way of the will that makes life to be sustained amidst the tensions and conflicts of the struggles which disrupt and give rise to chaos, and bring the world into order again. The man must choose in the way that keeps his or her mind mountain-bound. In acting he or she must gaze at Man-God, who is moving in the mountain path, where He is one with the whole and remains undisturbed. Teach man about the meaning of God-Man, who is one and the whole but still can remain individually separate from the rest. Knowing Him and the will of Man-God, your worldly appearance will be the source of actions that will determine the meaning of right and wrong. Know your will as the Will of God. Know Him as you and remain tranquil.

Christ-Man: In chaos and order, danger and disruption or joy and triumph, how can man remain tranquil and know the path beyond the path of worldly right or wrong?

God: God-Man is the meaning of life, and knowing the path of God-Man man must sacrifice his or her life without craving for the meaning that he or she may call right or wrong. God-Man is working in the mind of all. Knowing Him and the way He sacrifices Himself for man, man can keep the anarchy into control and move towards the whole where God is Man.

Christ-Man: Shall man step on the fire, sink in the water, or float uncontrolled on the tumultuous waves while fires, and flood will come in the life's way, or shall man seek a shelter or a vessel that will secure him against the fire and carry him across the tumultuous waves?

God: Man is a matter-spirit bound motion of a power that is manifest in form. Every man must undergo the tumults of the waves that change and move as the life proceeds. The waves, that you talk about, are the waves of the desires and attended by the will to move as a peaceless spirit that appears to be alone. Fire you mention is the fire of the matter-spirit burning as the fire in motion that is attended by the will of man. God is beyond such fire and waves, and does not exist in a form that is a worldly manifestation of the waves and the fire. Know the waves that are worldly and work against the forces that create tumults in the heart. Keep your mind gazing along the mountain path where Man-God is life's meaning and transcendent light of tranquillity and love.

Christ-Man: I want to know whether man must fight back the waves, that come to disrupt the home where man feels secure, or man must submit and let himself or herself be washed away?

God: Man is destined to undergo the tumults of the will and matter, that move in unison as a whole. Man can not escape this destiny. However, man can escape the feeling of suffering by receiving enlightenment. Resisting the disruption may work against the Will of God and thus against the way that can lead man to the higher path. Oppositely, in submitting to the forces one may end up submitting to the forces of the dark. Therefore man needs to keep in the vision the wandering of Man-God in the mountain path. By this process man will be able to stay in the desired path.

How to be worthy of Divine love?

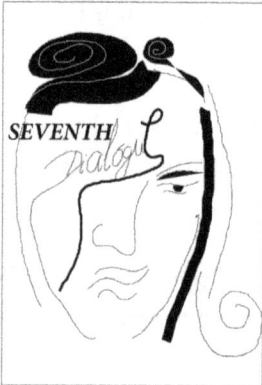

Christ-Man: O Heavenly Father! If it is true that I am Thy Son, bestow on Thy Son the blessings and the wisdom of Heaven so that I may be able to make judgements, and act and serve Thy purpose in a way that will make Thy Son worthy of Thy Love, like the way I love my son.

SEVENTH Dialogue

God: Bear in the mind that your son is a powerful incarnation of the will that is Divine. By the death of your son you are led to the path of the Divine. Bear in your soul the work of Man-God and work on behalf of the will that is God-Man. God is your Father and your Father wills Love for His Son. Born of man and woman you are worldly matter-spirit that is working for God. Know your desire is of man and will of God. Born of man and woman you are conducting this dialogue between Man and God who are not the same but united as One.

Christ-Man: O Heavenly Father! What will make me worthy of Thy Love that is so intense and Divine that I know by loving my son? Tell me the way I may win Thy Love.

God: Man-God is worthy of the Love of God because He is My Son. Your human aspect of existence is not worthy of the Love that you are seeking to achieve. The God-Man aspect of yourself is My Son, who is worthy of the Love that is Divine. Your human aspect is a man of worldly desire and anarchy of the will that sets man to act and move.

But your God-Man aspect is not driven by such power of the will of man. He rests in the Mind of God and God's Love is Him. Love your worldly son as you wish to love your God. God will love you the way you will love the world of Man. Born of man and woman you are also son of woman and man. Your love to your son is a love of the father, who is empowered by the same desires and illusions that constitute the life of worldly woman and man. Know that God is working for the Man and Man-God who are worldly and Divine. God's blessings are working for Man and Man-God as it works between Me and you. Read the Words of God from the realm of the Divine and know yourself as the Work of God - the Father who has created His Son. Know that you are Me and You at the same time, and you are working for the Love that I seek.

Christ-Man: Often I have felt polluted by desires and distress. The will of man has led me to fallibility of life that I wish to avoid. How shall I be able to reflect the Love, that you are, in the mirror of this soul that is covered with ignorance, passion and lust? How shall I be able to hold the glare of Thy Light in my body and mind polluted by earthly life's mire and dust? Tell me the way I must go.

God: Born of man and woman you are man of worldly matter-spirit and therefore your life is also bound to the world. This worldly life is a peaceless struggle against the forces of disruptions and chaos that are let loose from the beginning of life. Every choice, that you make, in order to live and move in life, is destined to encounter struggles and conflicts of passion and lust. Born of man and woman you are thus making yourself worthy of the love, that is man's and woman's love for the world. In the domain, where you are Man-God, there is no such man-matter-spirit's struggle and there is no will to move the world as desire. You are the worldly meaning of this search for God-Man. You feel polluted by the world because you are also man's and woman's son. But your soul is not born of man and woman, and therefore Light of God is able to penetrate your soul, which is Man-God wandering along the mountain path.

Christ-Man: I have felt disturbed by the trivialities of life that churn human mind like a darkness churning the depth of an abysmal night. I have resisted the forces of the night and struggled against the life to see Thy Light unveiled in the mind. In this search I have broken away and liberated myself from ties and bondage, that are so dear to human life, and thus taken upon myself the pain of not being able to share the sufferings of woman and man, who live in the tumults of life. What shall be my role? Shall I go down along the abysmal road and share the pain and suffering of woman and man without seeking Your Light, or shall I liberate myself from the darkness and seek Your Love and light, while man and woman will be left alone?

God: God-Man is the meaning of the world. Your worldly incarnation is the Work of God and you are working in order to fulfil the meaning of the Divine world that is not understandable by man. Your love for the woman and the man is working against the Will of God. Your love for the woman and the man is the peaceless world's struggle to move against the Light of God. God is not the matter-spirit-bound love that you conceive as a man of flesh and blood. God is a power that works in order to make the whole move in the domain of Light, that is not visible to any man but Man-God. The abysmal darkness, that empowers human life, is a power that resists the Light of God. The matter-spirit movements of the man and the woman are moving against Man-God. God-Man is the meaning for which they must live. Your love is not directed to man and woman, who live in the darkness of the soul, but exists in order to make the world anew, where man will be able to see the matter-spirit world as the Work of God.

Christ-Man: Should I remain aloof of the sufferings in the world?

God: Remain God-Man, who is attended by the Will of God. He is not a man and therefore He has no such will to love or love-not as you describe. The love, you mean, is desire-bound and works against the meaning for which the Love of God is directed towards you. You are not a peaceless world's matter-spirit soul. Therefore your life is not bound to the darkness where you see yourself existing in the bondage of blood and flesh. Your life is a powerful manifestation of God-Man who is working to make this world anew. Both as a God and Man you are the doomsday-messenger, who has appeared in the world of woman and man.

Christ-Man: What message shall I bring to the world? How shall I explain Thy Love that is different from the love of woman and man? And how shall I talk about the doom that will fill their hearts with sorrow and fear?

God: Man-God is the eternal peace and He is moving to make the world anew. Existing in the world above the earthly matter-spirit realm He is a power to set the world in the path of God and His Love. The world is working against this path and therefore your incarnation is the meaning of the world. Bear in the mind that after the doom your worldly existence will bring forth a new world, where there will be no war among the races of man. Your will will be one with your Father's Will, and your words will be the Words of the Divine.

Christ-Man: Where do you direct me to go before the onset of the doom?

God: Both as Man and God you are moving in the world among women and men. Both as matter-spirit bound and Godly existence you are existing as a powerful manifestation of God as Man-God. Both are working before the doom. Remember that your work is not the work of a worldly father for his son, but the Heavenly Father's work for His Son's death and resurrection. Death of the man will bring the resurrection of the woman-man born God-Man. O Son of Heaven! WORDS of WORDS are your words. Bear in you the existence of My Son. Father of Heaven wants your work to be fulfilled as the work of the formless world's work for the renewal of man. Go to the world and spread these words to the women and the men and ask them to seek peace in your Father's Words and the Words of God-Man.

Christ-Man: O Father! Let Thy Love be manifest through me, let Thy Light penetrate the world through me, let Thy Mystery be emanent in the consciousness of man as the mystery of God-Man through me. Move me the way you wish that I should move in the world, guide me on the way where you wish me to remain in the path of the suffering world. O Father! Let Thy Light illumine! Let Thy Love cleanse this polluted soul full of ignorance and empower it with bliss! Let Thy Mystery be unveiled through the body that I bear, and let my blood and flesh be sanctified by the resurrection of Thy Son in human blood and flesh! O Father! Illumine!

God: O Son of Heaven! God is reborn. Your Father is reborn as You. Your Father is nothing but You. Remain Me and be one with the Light that I am!!!

Walking along a destined path and man's fear

Christ-Man: O Father! I have heard you speak as clearly and unambiguously as no one would ever expect. Your voice has consoled; your answers have surprised; your presence has overwhelmed my mind with a certainty of the knowing that I have been hearing the voice of the Eternal Light. I have woken at the end of the night, bend my mind and felt the unearthly resonance flowing through my body and mind. When the morning has come and the daylight has penetrated the day you have remained unveiled through the Words, that have emanated from the Light. With the daybreak the senses have penetrated and entangled the mind like a web, which spreads chains of causes and effects. I have gradually lost the power to see the world that is beyond. In the light of the day, where the human life is engaged in the contest of power and competition for daily advantage, I have seen the great darkness. In this darkness I have been unable to speak to you and hear your voice as clearly as I have done before the onset of the dawn. The doubts have flouted through the heart; reasons have tried to rebuff all that I have heard; I have become a victim of the knowledge of the women and the men and all that are said or heard. I feel an anxiety to go to the women and the men and speak about my Divine birth. I am afraid, they will receive me with doubts in their hearts. Tell me how shall I perform Thy task?

God: When your words will be spread as the Words of God your words will transform as the matter-mind bound words, that are especially oriented to convince the doubtful hearts. When your words will be spread to the matter-mind bound world your words will be working to make the worldly men and women faithful to the Words of God-Man, who is the doomsday messenger moving on Earth. Your words will turn into a force that will change all that matter-mind bound world will try to discard with the help of reason bound to the earthly understanding of the world made of material dust. How do you go and how do you speak to the men and the women are something that you must decide. Speak to the world as you speak to men and women of your worldly counterpart. But remember the Words, that you are seeking to spread, are moving through the Mind of God-Man and He is working, moving and spreading the Words to all.

Christ-Man: When is the ripe time to bring your messages to the world?

God: Remember that you are God-Man and your existence is well planned. He is Man who will move and will make you move when the time is ripe. Your will is not able to decide the time because will is not what decides your existence and the movement of God-Man on Earth. Your will is the will that rests in God and God is the mover of your will when He deems your will to move from God. He is your Heavenly Father and the man, who is the worldly counterpart, will not be able to know when you move or move-not. Your work is My Force and My Force is making you work. How do you decide is not what I decide but what is decided is done by you by My Heavenly presence as the power of Words and the fate of man. Decide not what you want to decide. Decide what is decided by the Words of God and remain tranquil.

Christ-Man: Is it all pre-planned and predetermined?

God: God-Man is Man and God who are united as one. Your existence has a plan and in that plan you are not the one who decides what will be moving on Earth. I am the mover of the will that moves without the will of man. Predetermination is a concept where the preconception of the time is assumed. But in the predetermination of the type, that I talk about, there exists no time and time, is not something that can bring the concept of predetermination in the existence that belongs to Me.

Christ-Man: Is it all contained in Your mind, that can not be known?
God: Your concept of determination is derived from the down-fallen world's concept that is bound to the matter-mind. The determination, that you talk about, is a poor matter-mind world's movement that subjects itself to the laws governed by the moving forces determining the sequences of time. But determination has another concept beyond the matter-mind boundary and is not a concept that is workable in the domain of time and space. The determination you conceive is the work of matter-mind but the Work of God is determined by the Will that can not be determined by any concept based on space and time. Know that matter-mind world is war-torn movement of destiny that is seeking a peaceful resolution of the conflicts that make the world move. While determination has a meaning only when things are matter-mind bound, there exists a power that is not determinable and this indeterministic world is the world of Man-God, who is moving to Man and becoming one with God. Bear in mind that your deterministic fate is not determined by the forces of the matter-mind but by a power that moves beyond. Born of the matter-mind your body is seeing its image reflected in the sensory world where things have a predetermination within a boundary of movement. Bear that in your mind, and determine your acts according to the Will of God.

Christ-Man: Is my existence bound in Your Will and not conceivable by myself as a man?

God: Son! Know that your will is my will and therefore rest in peace in the Will of God. How do you know Me is not what your words can explain, and what you know of you is something that I can not explain. The human words are matter-mind bound and have limited power to penetrate the realm of God-Man, where no words are explainable by the words of the women and the men. Bear in the mind your Heavenly existence and seek not to make a meaning of yourself through the words of the world that can not explain the realm of God-Man.

Christ-Man: O unknowable! Inconceivable! I wonder why anxieties to go down and speak about the Divine still lurks in my heart? How shall I overcome this fear and walk along the destined path?

God: God is peace and rest in peace in God. Both as Man and God your mind is driven by the opposite aspects of the same Man-God. Both as Man and God your life is a movement along the worldly and the Divine paths. Move to the men and the women as Words of God and move away from the worldly men and women as the messenger of Heaven. Bear in your soul the Words through which I move and remain tranquil.

The fallible man and the mystery of God revealed

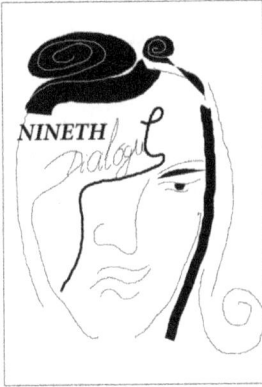

Christ-Man: My life too has been full of trivialities and tremors of the liking and the disliking like all others in life. I have been unable to remain aloof and tranquil to the situations while men and women around have demanded from me the codes of conducts, as from any other man or woman in life. No one in this world knows about the realm where I belong to the Divine. No one has ever come to know what has been going on inside the man, who looks similar to them and has been entangled in the trivialities of life. They have demanded from me, like they demand from all, attentions that a man must devote to the actions and the errors that determine the daily courses of life. I have been given tasks to perform, endowed with the responsibilities that I wished to avoid. But I have remained tranquil, hidden my nature and performed the tasks as someone hidden behind. At every moment I have confronted the choices of how to live in the world and at the same time remain distant from it. There have come moments when I have felt disturbed, experienced the burden to bear this mask. O Father of Heaven! How shall I remain tranquil? How shall I hide the mystery that I know? In choosing and acting in the world I have felt polluted: The love, that I desire from Heaven, I have been unable to transmit to life. Anger, frustration, fear have spilled on the heart. I have failed to control the eddies that have passed by as the whirls of the suffering-life.

If I am Your Son, why have You created me with such human attributes, that pollute the mind and do not let Your Light be revealed, twhich my keep the soul undisturbed? O Father! Knowing the nature of Thy Love I wonder why have You created me as a man, who is so small, and hurled me in the eddies, where I have swirled in the current of fallibility in the will of man?

God: Man is not God. But God is reincarnated as Man. Worldly man is a peaceless existence carrying the will of man, who is a powerful existence of Man-God. Both as a man and Man-God your existence is God-Man. Remember that unless you are dealing with the existence of the man, who undergoes the experiences of the trivialities of life, you will not be able to communicate about the World of God-Man to man, who are swirling in the eddies of life. Your existence needs to face the many-faced aspects of the common human life in order to be meaningful to yourself and the world of men and women, to whom you are going to be revealed as God-Man. But know, although your existence appears as world, and every worldly existence has a worldly fate, your fate is not a worldly fate of men and women. Your are God-Man.

Christ-Man: Sometimes I have felt that my mind is so polluted that I have been unable to receive the warmth of the love that I wish to transmit to men and women. At such moments I have felt the difficulty to belief that I am Thy Son. If I am Thy Son, why have I felt anger, frustration, liking and disliking for the situations of life that I have faced?

God: Know yourself as a man who is worldly and at the same time Divine. Knowing your worldly nature perform the tasks that are bestowed on you as the man of the world and remain calm. When the world will be imposing upon you the tasks that will hinder you to serve the Divine meaning, be assured that the Divine meaning will be established by the Will of God.

Christ-Man: How shall I be able to free myself from the unclean world and bathe in the Pure Light of Your Love?

God: Know that the world is full of torment and struggle. Know yourself as the part of the suffering world. Bear in the mind that the worldly suffering is the way to move to the world where Man is God. Your feeling of being polluted or unpolluted has a worldly meaning. Know that there is nothing that can remain untouched by the conflicts and struggles of life once the thing or the being comes in form. This is what must, and what must be is what you can not avoid. Reality of the world is a peaceless work of the will. Reality must and the worldly man must work for what is worldly and not what world should not be. Bear in your mind the meaning of God-Man, who is not a work of man and the world, but of God who is not a peace or peaceless light or darkness but the power of the Divine that creates all. Your earnings for the earthly world's purity of the love is not the earthly world's earnings for the attention of the will that is trying to work against the reality of things. Know yourself as the matter-spirit bound man, who is God-Man. God is a power of a world that is beyond.

Christ-Man: How shall I bear this will of man, that brings torments of passions, lust, desires, anger, hate and love? How shall I remain tranquil when I can not remain calm once born with flesh and blood? How shall I overcome the feeling of despair against my existence that creates turbidity of feelings that seem to be beyond my own control? The instincts operate without my willing or not; the desires flare up without giving warnings to the mind. How shall I overcome myself and attain self-control?

God: Do not leave yourself the doubt that you are not a man but God-Man. Once you know that your life is destined to be the way it is and emanent from God, you will not repent the way you seem to repent. Your repentance is a formless world's faceless man's understanding of himself as a man of the world, but not his understanding of Himself as God. You must not repent for what you do. You must leave your will to God and act. Bear that your will is not of a man, but God-Man is your Will.

Christ-Man: I have felt tormented by the human will, that has distracted me from the light that I have seen beyond. I have wished to remain submerged in the Great Light, that You are. I have repented for this separation from the Divine Home. When you have sent me to the suffering world to feel pain, anxieties, storms of passions and desires, you have a purpose, I know. O Father! How shall I go to the men and the women and tell them that through this polluted river, that fills my will, flows the river that is Your Home?

God: God-Man is a peace. This peace is not what man believes it to be. God-Man is a peace that disturbs the world seeking worldly meaning and awakens the world to the understanding of the Divine. Your worldly existence is not worldly peaceful or peaceless motion of the will. Your worldly existence is Man-God's meaningful work of the Will of God. Know yourself as the river from where everything evolves. Turn yourself away from the motion of the worldly man's willing and not-willing and deliver yourself to the meaning of the motion that is God. Know yourself as the meaning of the world, and realize your work as the work of a man, who is only knowable beyond the world, that is known.

Christ-Man: O Father! With my human will I have been unable to grasp the meaning for which I seem to exist. The language seems to have fallen in a dichotomy with itself: The meaning has turned meaningless. How shall I be able to make the messages meaningful to the men and the women, who do not know You and have not experienced the world, that I know?

God: God-Man is the meaning of the world. Your existence as the man is the meaning that every human being must understand. Your will is a power that manifests as a man and your will decides upon the meaning that is human. Know your meaning as God-Man and the meaning of your existence as the Will and Work of God. Knowing yourself as God remain attuned to the will that belongs to God-Man. Know yourself as God-Man and move and act as known and understood by man and remain undisturbed. You are working for the Divine world and work for the knowledge that is not known. Know the worldly man's feelings by living like them, and decide about the language that your worldly existence may find in the words of the worldly women and men, who are not you but who are aspects of you, who is the faceless and form-

38

less world's meaning as I and You.

Christ-Man: Lead my soul the way you wish to lead. Let Thy Words penetrate the suffering world through the words that I create. O Father of Heaven! Let Thy Words be the way!

The meaning of the world

Christ-Man: When I shall go to the world carrying all the weaknesses of a man how shall I convince the world that I am Thy Son, my home is Heaven, and I am one with You?

God: Your will is not God. This will is the part of the world and the world of your will is a part of My Will. Your will is not what you will. God is willing to work for world's meaning of God-Man and therefore your work will be the Work of God. Your worldly face is not what means anything to man; but what your worldly face is about is the meaning of the existence of God-Man. Your face is a form. But the face, that is beyond, is formless and Divine. God is you and you must not move as if you are a man. God has ordained your fate and you need not bother about the way I shall move as you. God has the world's fate in His mind and you are a face of God who is working in the world to make Him known.

Christ-Man: Why have I then felt affected by the will of man? If everything is ordained by You and nothing can be changed by my willing or not, why have I willed in the way every human beings will while choosing, judging and implementing the will into acts? Why is this illusion? How shall I overcome the illusory judgements, that arise from the will of man, and know that I have no will but I am one with the Will of God?

God: Bear in the mind that willing is a process of conflicts, that brings to man the movements of thoughts, and the coming and the going in the material sphere. But the Will of God is not conflict torn. It is the will beyond the matter-spirit world and does not belong to the world of man. Both as Man and God your willing is not a willing as a man, and not-willing as a man is willing as God. Your will is not fate-destined will of man but destined by God as the fate of the world. Bear in mind that your will is not what will is in terms of worldly meanings, which will may create. Bear in the mind that your will is a power to move beyond. It is an exotic peace in a peaceless movement of the world into forms, and by forming this world this will becomes what it is not. God is the will of the worldly Man and Man is God's worldly will as movement of Man-God. Bear in the mind that your will is a power to move, and beyond that movement there exists a power that wills-not. God is peace, and the peaceless work of Man-God is the Work of God. Both as Man and God your will is working to make Me and you as the parts of the Will of All. God is world's meaning. Both as God and Man your existence is the meaning of the world. Retain this worldly meaning of existence and remain in the world as Man and God.

Christ-Man: It is difficult to grasp in the language in which you speak the meaning that may make meaning to worldly man. I do not understand the inter-relationship of Man and God in terms of the words that can be meaningful. O Father of Heaven! I can not grasp the meaning that you talk about. How shall I talk about the meaning that I myself do not understand?

God: Both as Man and God your Will will be the meaning of the world. Bear in the mind My Will as God and your will as Man and move as destined. Both as Man and God your meaning will be understood by the world. Bear in your mind that your work is the meaning of Me.

Christ-Man: If everything You say is true, tell me why have You not endowed Your Son with the power that belongs to God?

God: God has a meaning behind your creation and therefore God has

41

made you the way you will act. By implanting on you the power of God to create or destroy the world as the acts of His Will will be against the meaning of the incarnation of God-Man. Both as God and Man you are worldly and Divine. Both as Man and God you are making the world as the will of Man and the Will of God, that is beyond.

Christ-Man: When men and women of the world will ask what proof do I have about my Godly existence, how shall I reply?

God: It will be erroneous for women and men to ask your worldly counterpart about your existence in the realm of God. You must correct the errors upon which they base their concepts of you and Me. Tell them that God is your Father and born of Father you are His Exotic Son, who is incarnation of God in the tormented world in flesh and blood. Because you are not Him but originate from Him your world is sorrow-stricken and divided into Man and God. God is a power that will be born as the Exotic Man after your will as man will cease, and you will be reborn after the world will be destroyed. God is peace and rest in God in peace. Do not ask Me about what I am, or I am not. Exotic existence of Man-God can not be explained by the words that can be grasped by the worldly women and men. Son! Do not ask the Exotic existence about you and do not establish in yourself both doubt and faith. Doubt not what I say and move as I have destined your fate.

Christ-Man: Why should the women and the men believe what I shall say?

God: Son! Your words are the Words of God and therefore women and men will be destined to face the Words that emanate from Me. Your words will be the force that will work for Me and the meaning of the world will be established through the Work of God-Man incarnated as you. Know yourself as Me. Know that they will be disturbed by hearing what you say, but knowing that you are working for God they will submit to the Words of God in faith.

Christ-Man: I do not know where shall I go and how shall I spread the words that I hear from You. I wish not to confront the world in turmoil. How shall I go in a world that burns in the faithlessness in God as a fire burning in Hell?

God: Do not move until I move you from where I am. Do not submit yourself to the will of man and do not go and preach the way as if you are created by the will of man. Do not seek to be what you are not. Seek in God your meaning and work for what is sought by God.

Christ-Man: Will You move me when the day will come?

God: Know that your will is already moving in the world as the Words of God. Enter not the fire before the words will be spread in the world through the poetic work that you have created. Know your Divine words and the poetry of God. Know yourself as the poet of God. Son! Do not move before I instruct. Do not seek path in the world and assume not your role as God-Man before I have formed the basis of the foundation of the new world through destruction by wars and cataclysms. Seek peace in God and let Words of God be fulfilled as the Words of God-Man.

Christ-Man: O Father! Let my soul not turn before you touch it with your fire; let not my mind aspire beyond what is destined. Give me the strength and wisdom to remain calm and see Your Will unfold as the meaning of the world. Let me see beyond, and see what is, and what is not, and stay close to my Divine Home. O Father! Let not my mind be moved by the illusions of the world and let my soul rest in You.

God: Both as God and Man you are moving in the world that is going to face destruction. Keep this in mind and move!

Doom

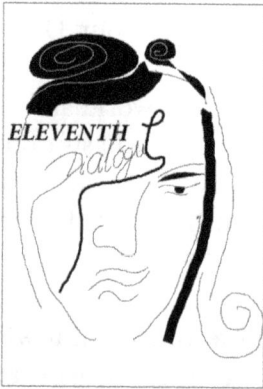

ELEVENTH
Dialogue

Christ-Man: You have talked about the doom. Tell me about this doom, that you say is soon to arrive.

God: Reality is what you see and feel and form following the process of the work of the matter-spirit, which is bound. But the unreal, that is not, is the reality of the world that moves as matter-point and energy in union and moves as the movement of the meaning in the world. God has sent Man-God as the doomsday messenger, who will work for the meaning of the world and make the world anew. Earth will be undergoing a violent cataclysm and the world will suffer from a movement of war that will make man shudder in fear. Doubt not that your work will be the world's end and beginning of a new world. Doubt not the movement of the power that is going to destroy. Doubt not that mountains will move, the world will be shaken by the rumbling of the mass that forms the world's crust. Reality is not what you believe it is. World is not in reality what you feel and touch. Reality of the matter-spirit is far deeper than what you can know by the senses. Doubt not that the mountains are already moving all around the crust, and soon they will erupt to fill Earth with mountain dust. My Will is working to make the mountains move and bring the destruction of Earth.

Christ-Man: When the mountains are going to erupt?

God: Doubt not the doomsday that is moving close. Doubt not the movement of Earth that has already set in the process for the day when all parts of the continents will be thrown into a turmoil of water, air, fire and earth. God has ordained the fate of Earth that will see its end. God will be reborn and then a new world will come. Get ready for the doomsday that will move as you will finish this dialogue between God and Man. Eruptions of the mountains will start, the water of the sea will bulge, the wind will bring hurricanes and massive streams will overflow the banks. Death will rampage the matter-spirit world and make man lowly and feel distressed. Doubt not the Words that move from the Will, that makes the mountains move, the weather change, and create death.

Christ-Man: Will the whole human race be annihilated ?

God: God is working to make the mountains move and by the movement of the mountains Earth will experience a cataclysmic destruction. Both the mountains and the seas will create havoc that is imminent.

Christ-Man: Will any human being survive this cataclysm?

God: Europe will be severely destroyed by moral chaos; Asia will experience massive mountain movements; Africa will be devastated by malnutrition, disease and death; America will experience the turmoil of the surge of water, wind, streams and severe heat and cold. God's Will will work to make Earth move towards massive annihilation that will eradicate much of the population. God's fearful words will be spread all over world and God will move as the Will behind all creations and the meaning of all life on Earth.

Christ-Man: How long this chaos will reign ?

God: The chaos, that will ensue soon, will be the fate of man. The sea will engulf shores, the eruptions from the mountains will make the barren lands fertile that will make the world anew. Europe will soon be engulfed into a cataclysmic man-made catastrophe. This will be world's fate in the near future.

Christ-Man: How long will this last? Will order regain?

God: God's Will is working for the renewal of man. The women and the men will be making a new world, that will no more be based on the understanding of science of the matter and the endeavours of man in trying to find the meaning of the existence in the material sphere. The destruction will be moving as a force to renew Earth. Once the matter-spirit world will be ready for a new world, that will move with the Will of God, the destruction will be working as the forces of order amidst chaos. Bear in mind that destruction is not chaos. The chaos brings a transition of the world from one state to another with the force that is uninhibited by the will of the man and out of man's control.

Reality is not what you believe it is. Reality has a Divine meaning and is governed by a force that is working to bring order and chaos in the movements that are worldly manifestations of the Will of the Divine. The mountains are moving as the results of the will that is working behind the order and chaos working in union with the whole. God's Will is not order or chaos. God's Will is world's meaning that is bound in world's order and chaos. Order is implanted in chaos, and chaos is the state before any order. Therefore the chaos and order are working together at all times. Both are worldly matter-spirit bound forces that can not be separated from the whole. Doubt not the mountains are going to make this order into chaos a reality soon. God's Will is working to bring the doom.

Christ-Man: Will human beings inhabit Earth after this renewal?

God: God's Will is to renew the world and its inhabitants so that the world will be a place for the women and the men who will be working for the Will of God. God's will is a force that has created the human beings as you see them now. But in the future they may not be the same. Doubt not that the mountains are moving to bring this transition to Earth. Death is fate of man. Man must work for God.

Christ-Man: Will this change come suddenly, or slowly with centuries or millenniums to come?

God: Death is moving to the world. God's Will is moving as a force to create men and women of the future. They will be reborn in a new world where God is the Will of All. Search in the Words the force that will make man understand the meaning of order and chaos. The process of transition to the new world will not be abrupt. It will work for world's renewal for many generations to come. Death will move and world will face its doom. With this doom a new life will start. Do not doubt My Words. Your Father has sent you to spread this message of renewal before the mountains will move and spread havoc on Earth.

Christ-Man: If the doom befalls mankind who will hear the messages You send with Your Son?

God: God's messenger is not the messenger for men and women who are living now. Your messages will be directed to the future when men and women will rise from death and destruction and work to fulfil the meaning of the Will of God.

Christ-Man: Shall I not also perish with them?

God: Errors of the modes of thinking of the worldly man create this false understanding of what you are. Your existence is imperishable. Your worldly existence is a matter-spirit manifestation of the Divine existence. You are My Son. Very reality in the flesh and blood is the worldly manifestation of the energy that lies beyond. It is a miracle that no one will ever understand. Know yourself as God, and make no association with the man, who is made of flesh and blood. Your Will will remain moving on Earth till the world will be renewed by your Divine birth.

Christ-Man: Let Thy Will move, let Thy Light penetrate the world, let Thy Words fulfil the meaning of the creation of Thy Son! O Father of Heaven! Let Thy Light illumine my mind before the onset of the doom!

47

God: GOD IS WORD OF WORDS. GO TOWARDS THE WEST AND EXERCISE GOD'S POWER ON THE EUROPEAN WOMEN AND MEN FIRST.

Christ-Man: Why?

God: God is forming the world as willed by Him. Go as I instruct.

Abysmal world, fate: Illusion of suffering

Christ-Man: Instincts of war, conflicts, competitions and the desire to gain power and advantage over others, that will make one's life secure at the cost of others, against whom man competes, seem to be the primary forces driving man to choose and act in life. Most human beings seem posed for battle against each other where individuals need to excel and defeat the others in order to enjoy the advantages that only power can bestow. In every level of social order this seems to be true. In greater and greater hierarchical orders as the social units grow from the small units like neighbourhoods, to the nation, and the world of nations, the same forces operate: People everywhere seem to be organizing themselves, taking advantages of the powers and skills to manipulate the available conditions in order to gain advantages over the groups over which they wish to establish hegemony and control. The smaller groups cluster to form a larger group when the power, as individual units, proves insufficient to overcome the threats of competitions from the more powerful ones. Through confrontations and wars among these groups a social order is erected, that is based on an institutional framework, which provides mechanisms of control and methods of containing and oppressing the opposing forces that constantly try to win against the governing forces. In every unit, starting from the world of the nations to the tiniest social unit - as in a group of families clustered in a neighbourhood - this tension and struggle are the prime forces giving motion to social life. Everybody seems to try to gain benefit and advantage for their own or the members of their families, who are dear to them. In this network of competitions and conflicts there exist codes of conduct, that reflect the codes and rules imposed by the ones that win and dominate. Every unit seems to be an ebullient spot. Once the power, that holds the social order shimmering but contained, is weakened it results into turmoil before a new social power gains upper hand. The domination seems to be the controlling mechanism against chaos. When the social behaviour is mostly governed by the instinctual needs, the conflicts are resolved through brutal physical power and exercise of violence. Man maims, kills, tortures others in order to establish one's power and hegemony. Large part of human life seem to be thus instinct bound. Is there any ultimate purpose and meaning in this social existence, where wars and conflicts are inevitable and always raging? Or, is it only an abysmal world of suffering where human beings are doomed to live in competition and struggle? Is human life only a meaningless struggle and suffering that has no end?

God: Born of matter-spirit every man is doomed to struggle and compete with the rest. The one, who is working, is not the one who is moving the matter-spirit world at the end. Doubt not the meaning that lies behind this struggle and suffering. Doubt not the world's force that is bearing the struggle and suffering in order to make this world a powerful manifestation of the Will of God. However, when the matter-spirit works and makes itself manifest as a will, as if it is not working to fulfil the Work of God, the will brings worldly suffering, and the struggle of man becomes the struggle to move against the purpose for which the will is created. There is a meaning. Moving against this meaning will lead to suffering. Doubt not what makes the world move; doubt not what works behind the movements of all; doubt not the movement of Fate, that is not what you think it may be. Doubt not about the Working of God. Doubt not the world's Fate as the meaning of God. God has made this world and the Fate of man is destined to move according to His will. Fate of man is to move as destined by God's force that makes all move. Do not make yourself a suffering man by making yourself a part of the will that moves against the Will of God. Doubt not God's manifestation in the world is world's fate, and worldly man's destiny is God's manifestation in the world of Man. Doubt not in the world's fate that works to make matter-spirit exist as the world.

Christ-Man: Should man remain engaged in the struggle and war of life, or seek refuge from this struggle and battle that keep human life engaged? How will you advise man to act so that through their actions man may fulfil the meaning of the Will of God? What is the best path?

God: Born of matter-spirit every man and woman must remain engaged in the world as destined by the Will of God. Know that the world is not driven by any power that does not arise from God. Know that the worldly appearance of the objects is not conditioned by a force that generates meaningless movements of the matter-spirit, that does not move anything in the inert world. Doubt not in the world's meaning in what the world is formed of. Know that the world is the Work of God. Knowing this, work according to the meaning that has made you incarnate as a part of God. Knowing that your life is partly human and partly issuing from God, remain engaged in the world where life is a struggle and suffering of the will of the worldly women and men. Doubt not that your incarnation as Man is the meaning of the world and in your worldly incarnation man and woman of the world will find meaning of life and thus understand the meaning of the human destiny. Know that the world's Fate is you and work for the fulfilment of the meaning of God. Working men and women will suffer around you. There are sufferings caused by the will, that moves against the Will of God. But remain calm against this force of the darkness that moves against the will that is trying to bring to the world the meaning and the fulfilment of the Will of God. Know that the world is moved by the contradictions of the will of Man and the Will of God. Knowing the Will of God, know yourself as the meaning of life and remain engaged in the struggle and battle. Knowing yourself as the one, who knows world's beginning and end, remain engaged in the world as a man of worldly existence amidst raging conflicts and wars. Know that the world is the path that must be traversed by all, who are born, and no one can ever escape. Knowing your Heavenly path work as a man and fulfil the meaning that will move the world along the Divine path.

Christ-Man: In the world how to remain unaffected by emotions that worldly women and men call suffering and how shall man participate in life and remain tranquil and realize the meaning behind all as the Work of God? What is the source of the darkness that moves as the source of the will that causes the experience of suffering? How shall man overcome the forces that cause this suffering, and keep man engaged in the life's struggles and turmoils?

God: Hear from Father of Heaven the meaning of the existence of man and his life. Know that the world is the movement of the darkness and the light. Once the darkness moves and makes human life a motion of the will, that is bound to the world of matter-spirit, and keeps him or her self-absorbed in his or her individual separateness, the Will of God moves and sets the force in action to make man work for the meaning that rests in God. Knowing that every life is a movement that moves in contradictions of the will that will and will-not, and the human destiny is the formless world's manifestation in form, keep in mind that will, that is spirit bound, is not the force, which creates the movement that emanates from the domain beyond the matter-spirit world. The will of man is worldly and has a worldly emanation from the matter-spirit controlled world. God's Will is a force that generates the will as well as the power that wills-not. Keep yourself engaged in the acts of the world as if you are working for the fulfilment of the destiny of man, and fulfil God's meaning by remaining engaged in the human fate. Knowing that all are subjected to meaning, that is not moving in the world but emanent in the sphere of the Will of God, remain tranquil in life's destiny, that is moving to realize the Self through contradictions and conflicts as Man and God-Man moving together in time and space. God's formless existence is moving as form in Man-God and knowing yourself as Him remain tranquil in thoughts that move and move-not. Both as God and Man become and become-not. How do you work when you work-not? It is a question tied to the matter-spirit world that can not be explained in words bound to the human thoughts. Both as worldly warrior and a Divine non-actor you are Me and You joined in Man-God who is the meaning of life. Both as the worldly and the Divine you are not where things are, and where things are not there, you are.

Bound to this contradiction your life is a manifestation of the MOVE-MENT that is working to fulfil the meaning that is working as the force of God. Remain engaged in the world as Man-God. Doubt not your movement as Man-God and remain engaged in the suffering of life. Christ-Man: Is suffering an illusion? If not, what is it then?

God: Suffering is a power that creates the movement of the world as will and matter-spirit. Know that without this suffering the will and the matter-spirit world will not exist. Suffering is a force that contradicts and this contradictions make the world move. Knowing this contradiction will not suffering, and disentangle yourself from the matter-spirit world. Knowing this suffering know that life is a movement of the force where wars and conflicts can not be avoided. Knowing this you must work, and through working you will attain the enlightenment about the higher path, where suffering is an illusion and as well as not an illusion: It is an illusion when man attains the understanding of the Divine and the meaning of the worldly existence. It is not an illusion when man understands himself or herself as the man or the woman, who are participating in the fierce battle of life without the knowledge that it is the destiny of every man, which makes the world exist through contradictions between the matter-spirit-will and the Divine magic and mystery of the world, that is beyond.

Christ-Man: Has this suffering any meaning beyond the fact that it is inevitable, and one needs to understand its necessity as the governing force of life?

God: God's force is the meaning of the suffering. God has created this illusion of suffering in order to make things move. Once the will attains the understanding of the meaning of God, the will ceases to suffer and the suffering appears illusory to an enlightened mind. God has worldly man's destiny in His Will to keep things exist and move. Know that suffering is a path to move towards self-enlightenment about oneself and God.

Christ-Man: Is suffering suffering then?

God: Suffering has a meaning only in relation to the world. The world is an arena of contradictions full of wars, conflicts and struggles among individuals against each other. In this context it is the force that makes man remain engaged in the activities from which there is no respite. In this way man experiences suffering as a force that makes him or her work and keeps him or her engaged in the battle of life. Suffering is not a suffering when man has been able to separate his or her will from the worldly arena and sees his or her will unveiled as God's Will moving through the world.

Christ-Man: O Father! Let sufferings be the worldly way.

God: God's movement is making you remain engaged in the world as a man of blood and flesh. Son! God's Will is moving as you and know your suffering is not what the suffering man thinks it is. Therefore suffer and suffer-not!

Christ-Man: O God! In suffering let me suffer-not; in wars and conflicts let me engage myself in life and engage-myself-not! O Father of Heaven! Let me remain reborn in the world while you are never born. O Father! Open the way to Heaven and let my soul remain tranquil in the suffering of the world where your Will is the destiny and way.

God: Son! Go to the world and make man understand this enlightened way.

The way to remain in the enlightened path

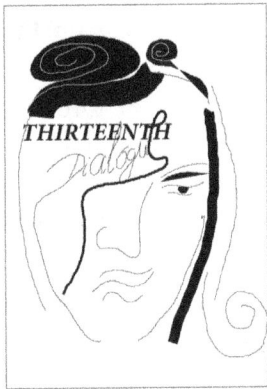

Christ-Man: Women have distracted the mind from attaining self-control and the perfection needed to follow the enlightened path. They have generated instinctual lust and attracted the senses and thrown me in the burning passion's hearth. While the passions have consumed, the mind has burnt in the fire and heat of the flesh and blood. This passion moves in the world all around. How shall I walk through this fire and remain tranquil?

God: Men and women in the world are created, as the two opposing sides of a dipole attracting each other, in order to form the world. Once born, the men and the women are destined to be attracted by each other as the Work of God. Once the body is formed the down-fallen world's force is generated in the body and the mind remains occupied with the desires that is directed to recreate the body itself. The worldly passion is the force that attracts man and woman towards each other in order to reproduce themselves in bodies made of worldly senses. Woman is the fate of man and man is the fate of woman. Both are the meaning of the world. Every existence inherits this dipolar unity that forms the matter-spirit world. God's Will is reflected in the existence of man and woman, that work in order to reproduce life. God is working through the process of death and birth. Both as woman and man know that this world is a Work of God. The fire, that consumes the body, is the energy that creates the world. Know this fire as the motive force that gives birth to the worldly existence. God has made it. Remain affected by this fire and know your sacrifice in the world. Both as Man and God remain burning and remain unmoved. Remain in the world as a man of flesh and blood and experience the force of the woman as the force of death attracting life away from the arena of God, that is not the work of woman and man. Assume the woman as the movement of life in the world in the other half where the world is working against the forces that wants to remain moving in the world of God. Every man and woman is destined to work in the world as two other-halves that do not work for the same purpose. One contradicts the other and thus makes the world move through contradictions of forces, that create the world. Know man as the force of the worldly matter-spirit that decreases the power of woman, and woman is the force that works against the force that creates knowledge of the conscious world. Woman decreases the light of contemplation and works for the matter-spirit force that makes the world move in the cycle of the death and birth. God has willed man and woman to work in this destined path. Remain working as destined for man and sacrifice yourself in the fire in order to bring enlightenment to man.

Christ-Man: Shall I embrace desire and burn in the passion, that woman generates, or shall I hold back and practice self-control?

God: Though you are born in human flesh and blood assume yourself not as a man of the world. Your role is different from man and woman of the world. Knowing that you are Man-God, who is incarnate in flesh and blood, choose to work for the force that works for the cessation of the world as woman and man. Knowing your Godly nature work for the force that creates and works for the Will of God. Assume the world as a powerful manifestation of Man-God and Man who are moving as unity in the world. Knowing yourself as the Work of God remain in the world of the woman and the man. Sacrifice yourself in the worldly fire and hold back when the fire will try to consume the Man, who is not a man but God. Existence must move and therefore lower your Heavenly state down and fall in the matter-spirit state and work for the movement of the woman and the man. Choose the matter-spirit world as the arena of sacrifice. Move, walk in the fire, but remain untouched. Desire you must; but desire not the desire that must desire annihilation through man's and woman's desire and lust.

Christ-Man: When woman will offer her love and desire to be consumed by passion that burns in the flesh and blood, how shall I act? How shall I walk in the fire and still remain untouched?

God: God's woman is not a woman of flesh and blood. Know yourself as the dual, who is partly woman and man. God's woman is a force that diverts the world from the matter-spirit world and determines the course of movement towards the Divine. Choose the woman of that Divine world and remain attached to the flesh and blood, as if, you are not a man of flesh and blood. Death is the force that appears with the consumption of love in flesh and blood. Once the woman consumes the body of the other-half the death remains active in the matter-spirit world by attracting the movements of matter into the domain of spirit that work together to annihilate itself and generate a new state that is matter-spirit bound. Knowing this, remain untouched by the fire that consumes flesh and blood.

Christ-Man: Should I offer myself to the passionate love?

God: God's Man is not a man of flesh and blood. God's movement as a man is not a movement of the worldly man who is passion bound. Knowing this, you are bound to work in the matter-spirit-bound world that is man's and woman's world of passion and the forces of desires. Offer yourself to the world where woman is not the woman of flesh and blood but the Divine woman moving along the mountain path. In the down fallen state when the woman will desire your bodily love as a passionate lover, do not submit yourself to the woman of flesh and blood. In the matter-spirit-bound world, when she will ask for love that generates matter-spirit-bound world by the process of annihilation and death, work for the movement of the world that is not the work of the desires of the woman and the man.

Assume not the instinctual man's role and do not seek the annihilation that follows after the consumption of flesh. You should not desire the down-fallen state of woman and man in the love of woman and man. Passion, that deviates the mind from the desire to love the woman, who is not passion-bound, but works for the man's movement towards the Divine light of love, is meant for the woman and the man, who are matter-spirit bound and work for the regeneration of the matter-spirit-world. The passion is generated by the woman's desire for the man. Your desire is not woman's desire for man. The down-fallen woman may will your love but submit your will to the Divine woman, who is your source of desire and love.

Christ-Man: Should I refrain from consuming women in flesh and blood?

God: Remember that you are not a man of flesh and blood. Your Divine world is not the same as the world where you experience the women of flesh and blood. The down-fallen state of the woman is not the woman who is your companion along the Divine path. Do not move to make love with the woman fallen in the instinctual love. You may ask how do you refrain from the women, who may offer you sexual love? Remember that the down-fallen woman is a woman who carries the death-like force that moves in the matter-spirit world. God's Will is working through her. Death is the fate of man. She is man's destiny: She brings man his death and gives birth to new life. Once you know her power and the matter-spirit destiny of man, you will be able to refrain from the desire that attracts man to woman as the force of life being attracted by the force of death. Remember that your existence is beyond this domain of life and death and your woman is the Divine counterpart of yourself, who is seeking love in the world. Refrain from the woman's love that brings death and life in the world. Born as a God-Man remain unattached to the world, where man's and woman's love and sexual hunger attract each other and are meant to destroy.

Christ-Man: When women will appear with her lust and passions, and desire sexual love, the instincts may flare up. It seems hard to control. How to control the instincts and remain in the fire without being touched by the forces of death and life?

God: Darkness is the force that makes man and woman desire love that produces the matter-spirit-bound world. Death of the world, existing in one form, is the source of life for another in a different way. This movement from one from the other carries on with the man and the woman desiring the darkness of the instinctual life. The down-fallen world is a powerful manifestation of the will that makes the world resurrect and die with the fire that burns as man's and woman's desires for death and life. This darkness is also operative when you are born as a man of flesh and blood. Therefore you too experience the same urges that no life can avoid. God thus makes the world move as the work of desire and love. Both as Man and God you are a powerful manifestation in the matter-spirit-domain and at the same time linked with the domain of God. Refrain from consuming the body in the matter-spirit bound instinctual fire and come to the Divine domain of Love. Your love as a worldly man is the down-fallen man's desire to move inside the boundary of man's and woman's love. God has made you and the woman in the Divine realm. You must remain moving in the path that is destined. Reality of your existence is what is unreal and therefore the woman is a virtual state of your being, that you experience as an unreal counterpart. Love not the woman who is the force of the dark. Love the woman who is the work of the Will of the Divine Love, who is moving along the mountain path.

Christ-Man: If I have understand You, the instinctual desire seems to be the harbinger of death. But it is also the force that brings forth new life. How should I understand the sexual world that creates and destroys?

God: Sexual man and woman are not the woman and the man that are working in you as the parts of the Divine person. The man and the woman, who exist in form, are the man and the woman who are moving without form in you. How do you understand this separation between what is sense-bound and what exists in the world that is beyond? Know that you are a powerful manifestation of the man and the woman without form. Knowing your Divine origin you must live as the man and the woman, who are the Work of God. Knowing the man and the woman as the Work of God you must work for fulfilling the meaning of the world. Knowing the world as your worldly manifestation as woman and man you will know the man and the woman as worldly work of sex and desire. God has made it and sexuality of the world is a force that makes the world exist. God has a worldly meaning behind the creation. So attract and move and move-not towards you and your counterpart. Move and move-not as woman and man. God has willed it so and God's Will is the force that makes you move and move-not as Man and God. God is and therefore sexual love is, and the Love that is beyond is also emanent in the world of death and life. Reality is a powerful manifestation of the woman and the man as God's world which exists as unreal and the woman and man are only working to fulfil the destiny.

Christ-Man: It seems very difficult to comprehend the movement of fate. Being a man of blood and flesh is it possible to understand this movement?

God: Fate is comprehensible only in the words that are moving in the world as the Words of God, that is moving as the power to make what is not made. God has the power to make man understand the matter-spirit-bound fate by moving as the words of Man-God. Your words are fate, and fate is your words' meaning. Death is fate. But death is God's meaning that has no meaning at the end where meaning lies in the words of the worldly man and woman trying to grasp the world as matter and spirit. God's Words are the Words of the movement of the force that is making the woman and the man move without any worldly understanding of the matter-spirit-bound fate. God's fateful movement is making you work for the worldly man and woman, who will understand your words as the Words of God, that are the source of fate.

Christ-Man: It is not possible to grasp what you say. Does fate operate through sexual love?

God: God's Words are fate. Sexual love is a force that creates and the creation has a meaning in the movement of fate. Your sexuality is not what is woman's and man's sexuality as governed by the cycles of death and birth. God's movement is your fate, and fate of the world is your movement in the matter-spirit-bound world.

Christ-Man: I can not understand the meanings of these words anymore. When everything are fated to follow the Words of God, how shall I understand what to renounce and renounce -not?

God: Born as a man you must serve the Will of God as Man-God incarnate in flesh and blood. God has a meaning behind the creation and He moves as fate of the world coming and going with Man and Man-God coming in and going from the world and the world which is beyond.

Christ-Man: As the mind ascribes worldly meanings to the words, that you say, everything seem meaningless. Tell me, while everything is already certain, whether I will or not, am I only a blind victim of fate?

God: Assume the Words as the movement of God in the world, and the Words of God are the movements of the Will that is moving without any connection with time and space. Therefore the words you use in order to understand the meaning with certainty in time and space are not the words that are moving to make the fate. Your words are not bound in the meaning of the words, that want to make the words meaningful in terms of the human experiences in time and space. Bound in the matter-spirit world your mind is working to make words meaningful in terms of the words that are worldly words of the sense-bound women and men. Bear in mind the Words that come from God and make yourself the Words of the formless existence that is not a matter-spirit-bound existence born of the worldly forces. God's Will has materialized as form and work to enlighten the man and the woman about the formless Divine existence.

Christ-Man: Aren't sex, birth, procreation, death also Divine acts? Why do you ask me to renounce the instinctual and procreative forces and move towards the world where there is no form? Why have you then created man in form?

God: Born as Man and God your existence is worldly and at the same time Divine. God is making Himself matter-spirit-bound through your incarnation as Man. However, your existence is composed of Man-man and Man-God, who are distinct as matter-spirit-bound and Divine entities, that belong to different spheres. God is not a man. God's powerful manifestation as Man is God-Man. Hear the Words of God and make yourself the words of Man-God. The exotic existence, that you bear, should never have been born; but once born, you have to move from the man and the woman and the matter-spirit-world. Son! The woman and the man, you see, are not your partners of love. Your companion is moving in the Divine world. Both as the Divine woman and man your words are the matter-sprit-bound world's destiny. Doubt not. Doubt not your Father's Words. O Man of Divine Birth! Know yourself as Me. Come unto me and be one with God!

The miracle of God and the dawn of a new world

Christ-Man: Why have you turned me away from woman? Why have you called the woman of flesh and blood as the darkness and asked me to move away from her? At the same time you ask me to remain living amidst all trivialities, weaknesses of feelings and follies of human life! Tell me how shall I grasp my role and perform my task in serving the Will of God?

God: Assume not yourself to be a man. Man-God is your counterpart in the realm of God. Know yourself as the Words of God. Assume the knowledge of Heaven and move towards life possessing the knowledge that you are an incarnation of Me. God has willed that you should move in the world as a man of common birth, who is indistinguishable from any other man. But by this process He has willed your existence to move as Man-God living in flesh and blood. Son! Words are moving to make you the power of Heaven that will create the world anew. Here and now the mountains are moving and soon the destruction will let loose. Knowing your force of words, that is moving to recreate the world, work for the Will of God. Knowing yourself as the Words of God, work for Man and Man-God.

Know that your are woman's flesh and blood and man's will. At the same time your flesh and blood is not the flesh and blood of woman and man. This miracle is not possible to explain. Your flesh and blood is the matter-spirit bound world's flesh and blood that make the matter-bound world move in the matter-mind-bound state of no matter and no mind, which lies beyond the knowledge of man. Know yourself as the matter-bound movement that is making spirit move in a world submerged in no matter and no spirit realm of the Will of God. I know it is difficult to comprehend these words. Know yourself as the movement of someone who is not moving and see yourself as the matter-spirit world's meaning as the Words of God.

Christ-Man: What is the meaning of telling me things that are incomprehensible and appear meaningless to human beings? I want to know why have you turned me away from the woman of flesh and blood and called her as the force of darkness?

God: Know yourself as the Words of God. Knowing the Words of God know the Work of God. God has created you for making His Words move through the matter-spirit bound human state. Knowing the power of these Words move to the matter-spirit state. Know that woman is flesh and blood's fateful movement in the darkness. Your existence has come down from Heaven in the darkness of the matter-spirit world. Your existence is working to liberate itself from the darkness of the matter-spirit. Know yourself as the incarnation of God in the darkness of the sense-bound world. Do not offer your worldly existence to woman's flesh and blood. Know yourself as the matter-spirit bound world's meaning as the Words of God. Move away from the darkness where you have incarnated as Man and Man-God. Knowing yourself as Man-man and Man-God work for the world's salvation and make yourself the messenger of the Words of God.

Christ-Man: Why is it so difficult to believe that I am You? If I am You, why so much doubt, why so much darkness and vacillation in accepting my Divine origin? If my existence is Divine, why am I not all knowable and why must I experience these conflicts and doubts in the process of knowing myself as You?

God: Son! Knowing is a process of the human mind that makes the words meaningful by associating meaning with the experiences of the matter-spirit world. Your existence is not bound to the matter-spirit and therefore the words fall in conflicts with the experiences of man and woman of the world. Your existence is also the existence of Christ-Man: It is the source of your conflicts. Know that your existence is a powerful manifestation of God as Man-God. God has willed your existence and therefore you are willing to know both as Man-man and Man-God. Knowing yourself as Man-man your life becomes conflict torn. But as Man-God your mind is moving beyond the realm of time and space. The knowing, that you point to, means the knowledge of the world which senses can grasp. But the knowledge of Heaven is not something that is understandable and comprehensible by the matter-spirit-bound mind which, in order to extract meaning, makes association with the world's movements as the matter-spirit- death and life's movements. Doubt is the power that attracts the motion of the matter-spirit-bound thoughts towards the meaning that is comprehensible as the matter-spirit bound world's meaning, associated with the senses and the logic of the cause-effect-bound process. The knowledge, that you wish to gain, is a fateful world's knowledge. God has willed that your knowledge will be the knowledge of the world that is to come. Your existence will be the meaning of the new world. The knowledge, that you ask to gain, when you desire to be all knowable, is the matter-spirit-bound knowledge that is not the knowledge of Man-God. Gain knowledge of the mystery behind the matter-spirit world's working force that creates You and the Words. Knowledge, you must know, is the knowledge of your Divine origin. Know yourself as a part of Me.

Christ-Man: Is there no knowing in the Divine world in the way man desires to know?

God: The road to the Divine world is paved by the Words of God. Knowing these words allows man to move towards the meaning of the man-matter-spirit world. Knowing the words of Man-man and Man-God there rises a force that makes man and woman of the world know about God. As I told you before, the knowledge of the world is a fateful world's knowledge and it works to make the mind fate-bound. Boundary of the Divine world lies outside. Knowledge has no counterpart in that world. Although you are existing both as Man-man and Man-God the knowledge, you seek, has meaning in the movement of Man-God. Know yourself as Man-God. As Man work to bring meanings through the words that are matter-spirit bound. God has no meaning the way Man may wish to associate a meaning with Him. God-Man is the meaning of man and God is the meaning of the world.

Christ-Man: Why do you call the sense-bound world as the darkness-bound sphere? Describe what is beyond.

God: Boundary of the senses define the boundary of the matter-spirit-cause-effect-limited world. Within this boundary the motions are created by the union of the matter-point and the energy, which, through contradictions, give rise to the form of the world. God has no such matter-point-and-energy association. He is beyond the motions of things. God is the power of the Words that generate the forces that move the world created by the duality of the matter-mind or matter-spirit. Your human body is created out of this process and thus you have sunk in a down-fallen state where the matter-point is cause bound and makes the movement of the energy making it possible for the world to manifest. Both as God-Man and Man-man your existence is worldly and at the same time Divine. Son! Soon you will realize the motion of God-Man and understand the realm that is beyond. To describe this realm in a language understandable to man is beyond the capacity of the matter-spirit bound words, that can not express the mystery of the world, which is not cause-bound. Knowing yourself as the Divine being describe the world as yourself in motion and no-motion. It is not visible, not perceptible. It exists in the sphere of the Will of God, that remains ever unknown. Your words are the only way to make Me known to the world. Know Him as you and know you as the Words of God. God has no other way to describe Himself to man except as you. Doubt not the Words of God. Doubt not the Words that are emanating from the Will that is beyond. Doubt not the Words that move and move-not. Cease to work and cease-not. Do not make words that are not the words of the world. Death and life is you and your life and death is the Work of God. Son! Darkness of the world is a fate-bound sphere of the matter-spirit tied to motions. Darkness means that your life is moving in the worldly arena where matter and spirit are moving in union and have no power to attain the enlightenment that can reveal the realm of God. Darkness means that the worldly vision is attracting the material motions in the arena of the senses and there is no-motion of the will that works for God. God has willed so. So will be the world. Know the movement of God, and death and life as the fate of all. Doubt not the force that is making you move. Doubt not the Words of the world's Saviour, who is incarnate as Man-God in you.

Christ-Man: O Light of Heaven! It sounds pessimistic and dark! Why all are thrown in the motions by Your Will to live in an abysmal darkness without possessing the power to see the Light of Heaven and understand the Meaning of Life? Can this blind man achieve enlightenment and find meaning of life and see Thy Light unveiled? What is the way?

God: Assume the working of God through Man-God and move in the world. Your words will make man and woman achieve enlightenment about Me. Your life is the only way that can help man and woman understand and see the Light of God. The world is a process that must go on and the life must follow death and vice versa. There lies attraction of the parts of the dual towards each other and no life can surpass this attraction of the opposite forces that hold everything in turmoil. Death and life is a must as the fate of the down-fallen world, that has risen in form. Son! Doubt not the working of the matter-point and the energy that couple to form this world. They contain the forces of death and life acting against each other in order to form and destroy. Doubt not what you hear. Death must and the working of life must end in the work of death at all stages and in all forms of life. God has willed so and therefore knowing God's Will be attracted and destroyed. Death, doubt, matter, motion etc. are all parts of the process that are world and, even if, you know the matter-spirit world's working mechanism there is no way you will be able to liberate man from this motion where God's Will is manifest as the power of death and life. Knowing this, doubt not what I say: Earth is soon going to face its destruction and the world will be renewed. God is forming the matter-spirit world as willed by Him. God has made it so, and so will be the world. O Son of Heaven! The darkness of the man is not anything pessimistic as you may believe. How will things move without the bondage of all to death and life? God is the world's fate and thus God's Will is born. How do you work and how do you save man and woman from the darkness and lead them to Light are the motive aspects behind the understanding of Me and how to make life meaningful by working for Him. Son! You will soon know your Godly motion and knowing that you are Me, your doubts, conflicts, pessimism etc., associated with the worldly life, will cease. God is not willing or not-willing. It is so, and so will be the world. Knowing the world as Him work for the Will, that God has implanted to fulfil the meaning of life. God must. Doubt not what I am. Doubt not the Words of the Saviour, who is working for the enlightenment of woman and man. Doubt not God's formless formation as the Light being emitted from the mind of Man-God. Soon the world will know my nature. Know that the world's Saviour is working for man and the world's meaning. Door of Heaven is opening for Man. Ask not. Vacillate not. Doubt not. O Eternal Poet! I am your Father. Your words are going to create a new world. Believe what I say. Go down and tell man and woman about God and His Son.

Enlightenment and liberation

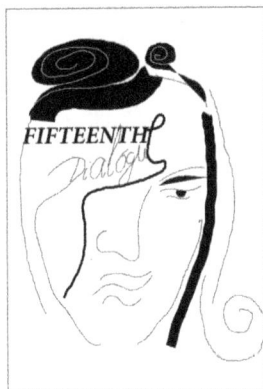

Christen-Man: Before I go down to the world bringing Your messages, although you have told me before, tell me once more in a language that is easy to grasp, about the forces that hold the instinctual life in motion. What is the meaning behind this motion and what drives man to choose and act in the arena of life full of struggle and conquest? People may ask what is the right and the wrong path? When they will seek guidance to move towards the enlightened way where I should direct them to go? When they will wish to know the way to escape from the suffering world, which advice should I give?

God: Know that you are God-Man and you have appeared as a person in the suffering world to make man understand the enlightened way. The enlightened path goes through the world of man and God united in life and death. Your are both worldly and Divine and the Divine is working through you to make man understand the downfallen world's motion and matter-spirit-bound world's fate. Your work carries the force of the Divine world and it is the meaning of the world. You are bound to Me but at the same time your worldly manifestation is moving in the worldly state according to the matter-spirit-bound destiny. This worldly manifestation is making life and death possible as the motion of the matter-spirit- bound world. You are making yourself moving by the force that emanates from Me. By the motion of the matter-spirit-bound world your worldly state is moving towards Me. Your matter-spirit-bound manifestation is working for the matter-bound spirit's liberation from the mechanized movements of the world. You are moving in order to move-not. You are working in order to work not. You are sound and light while you are moving outside the boundaries of perceptions that create sound and light. You are working as the movement of Man-God but you are not Man, but God. Your will is not what man will or will-not. Your will is making the world move and move-not. Your work is generated by the force of the willing, but not-willing is the motive of the willing to work. Your work is the motive force moving the world, but your motive is not-to-work. Your world was, is and will be bound to matter-spirit and its motion, but your will is not bound to the motion of the world. God is working as Man and man must work for God. Your manifestation is the motive force and the matter-spirit is working to make My Will manifest. Work and remain engaged in the world as Man and move as the force that is seeking to free itself from the matter-spirit bound estrangement and the force of life and death. Work for the matter-bound world's liberation.

Christ-Man: Has the world sprung from You in the arena of the will and matter-spirit bound destiny, where man must will in order to free oneself from the will, work in order to liberate oneself from the destiny-bound matter and spirit, choose and act in order to liberate oneself from the motion of the world? How shall I understand this contradiction? How shall I explain to women and men about these incompatible and opposite concepts as one, that is hard to understand?

God: Working does not issue from a force that is generated from the void. Working is the willing of the matter-spirit-bound world's fate. Know that by working the will works in fulfilling the fate of the matter-spirit-bound man's and woman's life. Working issues forth from the force of the matter-bound-spirit's working that make man and woman destined to follow estranged paths. Willing to liberate oneself from this path is willing to move in the arena of Man-God. Willing is the motion of the matter-spirit as destined by the forces of death. Escaping

70

this willing is the willing not to follow man's and woman's destined fate. Working is the fallen-world's matter-bound motion and working to free oneself from this matter-bound world is the will of Man-God. Man's will creates force that makes man estranged in the world of the matter-spirit-bound fate. Willing to act by using the will of man is willing to move as the matter-spirit-bound force of destiny. Will is not-willing when the will supposes Man-God as the will behind all acts. Man-God is not willing because His Will is not fate-bound. How do you move and how to make man move according to the will that moves and moves-not is a miracle that can not be explained. How do you work and work-not, how do you make and make-not, how the world is and is-not in your willing that wills-not, is something that you will not be able to explain.

Christ-Man: If man's and woman's willing are bound to the matter-spirit-bound destiny how shall man understand the meaning of choice and free-will? In willing and choosing does one bind oneself to the destiny or can man free oneself from the hands of fate?

God: Fate is moving through the will that is moving the matter-spirit-bound world. Force of the willing is the force of the destiny, that makes man and woman will the way they choose. The destiny is the worldly manifestation of the will that is moving to make the world matter-bound. Knowing the will, that moves and makes man bound to the matter-spirit-world and is making man and woman work against the Will that is above the fateful world's motion, make man and woman work for the Will of God. God-Man carries the will of man, who is moving to God. Knowing the working of God-Man, who wills and wills-not, ask the women and the men to move as you instruct. Knowing the worldly and the Divine, as Man and God, will and act, will-not and act-not.

Christ-Man: What is the meaning behind this motion of the fateful-world and the motion of God-Man and God? How shall man understand the meanings of his or her acts? How to choose? What is the right path?

God: Know yourself as Man-God and will and will-not. Knowing your worldly and Divine nature move to the world and make man and woman of the world understand the meaning of your manifestation as Man-God. Your working is the meaning of the world. By following your worldly and Divine movement through willing and not-willing, man and woman will realize the Divine meaning behind the creation. Knowing yourself as God-Man, make the worldly man and woman move in the fateful path as the matter-spirit-bound creation. Knowing the worldly and the Divine united in Man-God, make man and woman of the world will and will-not. Son! God has sent you to the world to make woman and man realize the mystery that moves and moves-not. Soul of Man-God is moving in the world as the Saviour of woman and man bound to the fateful destiny-bound matter-spirit world. Knowing the will that wills-not, make man and woman serve the Will of God by moving in the path illumined by Man-God.

Christ-Man: What is Your Will? Why things exist as they are? Why destiny? Why fate? Why matter? Why spirit? Why do You Yourself exist? What is the goal? Is there any ultimate end? Is there any ultimate answer why the will impregnates all and all are bound in the destiny of the matter-spirit-bound fate? Why man must liberate oneself from a state in which he or she is thrown, which he or she has not himself or herself chosen, and for which he or she himself or herself can not be held responsible? Why have You created me while You have created the world that wills and falls in the matter-bound state and seeks its annihilation by its own will and choice? Tell me is it a game? Only a tragic play ?

God: Born of matter and spirit your form is the world. Bear in mind that your form is the worldly manifestation of God. Searching behind the form you enact the will to move beyond the domain of the form. Son! Searching your own nature in the formless world you create yourself in form. Your formless existence is behind the worldly matter-spirit-world's force that creates the world in form.

Christ-Man: Father! Give me answer to the question I have asked.

God: Son! The world is the movement of you and Me in union as the worldly and the Divine. The worldly aspect is form-bound while the Divine is beyond form. Without the existence of the matter-spirit-bound will the matter will not come into existence and there will be no existence in form. Son! The world is formless and also has form. God is moving in the world as the formless force behind all forms. God has willed the existence because existence is the will that has made God emanent in the world. I exist without any form. In that sense in the world I exist-not. In existence I am non-existent; in non-existence I am existing as the formless motion of the Will who is God. Making the forms in the world I have formed a matter-spirit-bound world, where matter and spirit are destiny bound. Without the creation, I am "non-existent" and formless. To reveal me as emanent in the world the world has to be created in forms. By creating the forms I have moved away as the force of the Divine that acts and works as the Will of God. By willing to create the world I have worked against the formless world and separated Myself from the realm of God. Doubt not that I am worldly and the Divine manifest in the world as Man-God. Know yourself as Me and see yourself in the mirror of the universe. Knowing the will that forms the world and the forms that create the forces that seek to go beyond the forms see yourself as an inseparable duality in which your existence is bound. By moving I act to see Myself in the world as emanent and in form. By remaining tranquil I see My formless state in the void. There is no meaning beyond what is. God exists as emanent and matter-spirit-bound, and transcendent as formless and void. By existing I make the world meaningful as God's arena of movement and fate and worldly manifestation of the movement of God as man. Assume no other purpose but the world is Me, and I am behind all. Doubt not what is, and what can not be non-existent as long as the boundary of the matter-spirit world is not annihilated by the motion of the Will of God. God works to bring the existent beings to the realization of the oneness with God. God moves and therefore the world is and the world is therefore God is moving to make man go beyond. Know the world that is-not. Son! Know yourself as Me and know that the world moves according to what I will through You. Son! I am the whole; I am inseparable from all. It is Me who is and all others are my parts. See Me as emanent in the creation in forms. Return to me and emanate in form from Me. How shall I create Me without Me, and for someone else when everything are included in Me? Man must know that you are world's Saviour and they are your parts. You should tell them about your worldly and Divine nature and ask them to follow your enlightened path.

Christ-Man: If you are behind all and everything are your parts, what makes man fall in the darkness of the mind and choose the paths that contradict Your Will that wishes to make man realize the oneness of man and God, and the unity of all in form and no-form?

God: Your will works as the fate-bound world's will because this is the way the existence of forms can be sustained. Although form is the world, the formless world must move to accrete the form, which carries the will and becomes one with what is beyond. The form seeks in the formless world the movement of the will that will bring order in the world, that is being constantly disrupted by the will to free the forms from the matter-bound state. Thus the worldly will seeks to choose the fate by seeking to organize itself around orderly forms. By doing so the destiny moves. God's Will is not to bring an end to this destiny-bound world falling into the matter-spirit state but to make the will work against the matter-spirit-bound will that wills to destroy the order of the fate and the motion of the world that moves in and outside the temporal and the non-temporal domains.

Christ-Man: If all are your parts how does this conflict of the will, that contradicts, arise?

God: Son! God has no will and therefore there is no conflict of Will of God with any other will. Willing is the force that forms and by forming the will it becomes separate from God and moves in the destiny-bound path. When the destiny-bound movement works against the will, which wills to move to God, the contradictions move and the conflicts appear. So will is not the Will of God, but will that impregnates creation that is emanent from God. The emanent is not what is-not. And what is-not, is what I am. I am your Father. Your existence is the motion of God-Man, when willing and no-willing appear. Son! Willing is a mode to act and by acting one may separate oneself from God. God-Man is the path to follow in the world.

Christ-Man: Are you separate from the world of will and contradictions, or are you one with it?

God: Assume yourself as a part of the world. But not Me. Your world is Man and God. But when you are Me you are not Man but God. Both as man and God you are one with the world as well as separate. Doubt not the Words of God. Both as Me and the worldly man your form and formless existence are world and will. Son! assume your work and make man move in the path as You and Me. God is. So You are. Move as I instruct.

The magical movement of God that is revealed through man

Christ-Man: To whom shall I bring these messages?

God: Son! Go down in the world as a common man and move among women and men as if you are one of them. Words will be heard by your worldly companions when they will encounter you as a man. Both as man and God you should move and make your companions realize the meaning of your movement as a man of the world and the movement of the Words that come from Me. The words will be moving with you and through these words you should make man realize that they are parts of you. God is moving with you and know your words as God's movement in the world through you. Knowing God, move to the world and speak to the women and the men. God will make you indistinguishable from them so that they will not know who you really are. Both as Man and God you will know God's purpose and move to make the world anew. Knowing your movement as God, work to fulfil the will that is moving to make you the founder of a new world. Go to men and women and move amidst them without making man realize the truth that you yourself is God incarnate.

Christ-Man: Without revealing My true nature as You, how shall I talk about You and how shall I speak as if I am not You?

God: Doubt not my magical movement. I am not matter-motion

bound. Therefore I know all meanings of the words that will leave no doubt. Knowing your magical power to enter and exit the world as Man and God, you should move as if you are God and no-God. God will make you indistinguishable as a man when He will move in the world as you and make you incarnation of God - His Son - when the movements of the words will make man and woman realize themselves as parts of you.

Christ-Man: Why do you send me in disguise? What makes you play this role of Man when you are God? Why don't you reveal yourself in your true glory and let men and women see who You really are?

God: Doubt not my formless existence. I am not visible in form. God-Man is the movement of God when God incarnates in form. Existence of God-Man is matter-spirit bound and moves in the arena of God as well. Knowing you as indistinguishable from them, the men and the women will know themselves as the parts of Man-God, who is worldly and Divine at the same time. Road to Me is a movement through you. Existence will not be understood if I appear as non-existent and do not reveal Myself as you. Disguise you must wear because, if not disguised, seeing your existence, that appears matter-bound, men and women will mistake you as someone moving among them, who is different. Knowing you as one among them they will know Man-God as their Saviour and they will move in the path enlightened by the Words emanating from God. My true glory is not visible to any man but Man-God, who is the world's Saviour and through Him I reveal My glory to women and men. Knowing Me as Him and Him as Me, the women and men will know the glory of God incarnate as Man. Knowing My incarnation they will know the world and gain understanding how man and God interact. God is outside the boundary that is matter-spirit bound and remains inaccessible to the existent beings. Through you I am ema-nent and through this emanation in form I am moving in the world as Man-God. I am the world; I am Soul; I am all. You are my worldly movement. Distinguishing yourself from the world is not where I can be seen; I am visible where all are visible in forms. I am invisible where and when I am not existent as the world in forms. Doubt not My move-ment as exotic motion of God-Man attracted towards the matter-spirit bound world's movement in forms and destroyed by the motions of the Will of God. I am emanent and transcendent through you. God-Man! Move as someone indistinguishable from the world as My Son.

Christ-Man: Men and women carry the image of You as the light and the power supreme. They may not believe the messages I carry to the world unless they see God revealed in His incandescent and fearful form. Disguising as a common man how shall you reveal your power that maintains over all existing beings its supreme command?

God: Reality of the world is matter-spirit-bound. Know that the light and the energy that man imagines as emanation from God, is a worldly manifestation of Me in form when I separate from Myself as the Creator separating Himself from His creation. Know Me as the Supreme but do not imagine that I am the light and the energy that flow through and animate the world. Instead know Me as tranquil and serene. I am the motionless in motions. I am the world where there is no -world, no-form - no emission or extinction. I am the Supreme that is not willing to move but still creating all motions in the universe. Every beings are making cyclic rebirths from one state to another caused by the destiny in which the matter-spirit is bound. The image of God as fearful incandescent infinite fire is not what God is. God is the "fire" that remains within all fires as non-moving and eternal. This serene "fire" draws the emanent world to Himself and lifts all towards Him. Know Me as the compassion that has created all. Know me as the Love that impregnates all creations. The man and the woman of common birth are world's flame and through these flames I am emanent in the world. I am working to lift them towards Me. As the exotic Father, I am drawing them towards My Love through the creation of My Son. Be one with the world. Know Me and you as the Compassion of the world and serve the Will of God. Know that My power is most radiant as the power of Love. Love Mankind and make man realize My Compassion and Love. Be ordinary. Be world's Saviour. Be what Love can make in lifting the world towards Me. Be radiant in the world as the movement of the One, who is not fiery but tranquil Love that ignites all flames.

Born as Man and moving as God hear your Father's Words and follow His commands.

Christh is and Buddha becoming

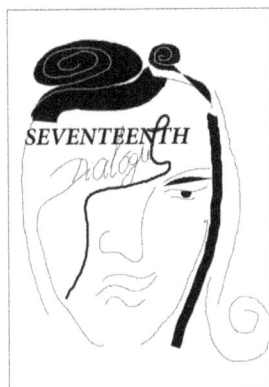

Christ-Man: The men and women have different concept of Son of God. Some believe that He had appeared before and died on a cross. After death he had resurrected from the grave and then had gone to Heaven to occupy His Heavenly throne. He will return again to resurrect the souls of the dead who will enter the blessed City of God. With his coming the disbelieves and the corrupts will be thrown in a pit to burn in the flames of Hell. Men and women, who is brought up to believe His return, think that He will descend from Heaven for the Salvation of man. Others believe in no such Man-God, who is a person and an incarnation of God. Some believe that God is nothing and the void and can never be known. According to them all are bound in the wheel of life and death, that ceaselessly turns and creates the sufferings of the world. By being born and reborn in life after life and practising in each life the right way of thoughts and conducts man may transcend this suffering world and escape the wheel of destiny in which everything are bound. Through multiple cycles of birth and rebirth man may attain enlightenment about the ultimate void and at the end will not return in the cyclic motions of life and death. The right way and the right conduct had been preached by a Sage, who had attained enlightenment. His existence is multiple and not conceivable as one particular person as a man. He is many in one; and in many-fold appearances in the world He is emanent as the guiding Light towards the enlightened path. He is

Buddha of the past; Buddha of the present, and Buddha of the future. By following this path man will be able to transcend the suffering world and become one with the one, who is multiple in One, and thus return to the void, from where everything have come. In this belief, God is dissolved in the void and Buddha as a person is Buddha in all persons coming and going while being bound to the wheel of death and life. To all these believers what shall I tell? How shall I explain Your mystery when they believe that their concepts of God are true and all other concepts are erroneous and false ?

God: Reality is moving, and in the real you are unreal. God has acted and you are born as the moving reality of God. Your birth is a powerful manifestation of the movement that is attracting the world to Itself as the power of God. Assume, without worldly understanding of your worldly manifestation, that your work is the Work of God. God is the maker of the whole, and the whole is made without the parts. The parts, that you are, and your worldly manifestation may resemble, are not your parts, but parts of the matter-spirit-bound reality, that moves and makes the world moving in the wheel of death and birth. Your worldly manifestation is working as the multiple movements of women and men, but you are not women and men. The multiple mirrors, in which the mind gazes at itself and sees its own appearances reflected in the world as reality, are the mirrors of the worldly parts, that are moving and making the wheel move in space and time. How to explain this to women and men, who believe that they already know who is God and who is not? Both as Man and God your appearance as a person and your movement as one of them will be making them realize the matter-spirit-bound world's movement in God. God has created you to make man understand who is God and what makes Him appear as a person. Though He is a person, that may appear worldly, He is not what they may believe He is. He is worldly manifestation where world is manifest in form; He is void where the world is not manifest in the worldly forms. Both as a person, who is manifest in form, and the will that emanates from the void, He is the world and the will as a person and the void. God is both. He is a person when He acts on the matter-spirit world to make Himself moving in the matter-spirit world as a manifestation of the Will that emanates from the void. God is an unchanging state that rests in the void, beyond will and form, when He is not manifest. Both will and will-not are states where God is. Both as world and will He is and is-not. Both as will and no-will He is and is-not. Essence of God can not be known because God is not the essence that is emanent in form but God moves as the force bringing forth the matter-spirit world's essence that appear in forms. Bound to the matter-spirit the world is moving and this moving world is the source of the illusion that negates the essence of the world that exists behind what is seen and known. Bound to the movements of this reality the men and the women can not know Me, who does not move. God is only knowable through God-Man, who is moving and not-moving as the worldly manifestation of the Divine. The concept of God as a person, who will descend from Heaven in physical form, is a worldly concept of the women and the men, whose visions and thoughts are matter-spirit-bound. Know yourself as the movement of God and His appearance in the world as envisioned by women and men. Enter and exit the world. Work and move as God's messenger, who is the Saviour of the world that is matter-spirit-bound. God is not what they presuppose God should be. I am not what I am imagined to be. God is and is-not. God moves as God-Man, who is the worldly incarnation of the Will that makes the world to be. I am emanent as God-Man, who is a person and worldly when He is emanent as the will of Man, but He is God when He is transcendent and exists beyond the boundaries of will and forms. I move without moving; I incarnate; I make Myself matter-spirit bound while at the same time I remain unbound and untouched by the motions of the matter-spirit forms. Entering the world I remain beyond, and without form and exiting the world I work to bring forth forms. God-Man is my way to enter and exit the world in motion and form. The existence that descends from Heaven is not existing in form before I emanate in the world as God-Man taking man's and woman's form. Assume God-Man as the matter-spirit bound world's movement where God is incarnate but not one with the form. God is a person when the Will of Heaven descends and incarnates as the matter-spirit-bound man. He is world's Saviour and world's meaning. The belief that God-Man will return in flesh and blood is the matter-spirit-bound women's and men's concepts of God as a man, who is flesh and blood. Both as flesh and blood and worldly matter-spirit-bound man and the matter-spirit-bound world's Saviour, who is not moving in the matter-spirit-bound state, He is God-Man. Enter and exit the exotic state and the worldly arena and show to the women and the men that God has incarnated in the matter-bound state without being bound to the destiny of the world that is bound in the matter-spirit-world's fate. Assume yourself not to be Man, but God born as Man, who has entered human blood and flesh. Though born of woman and man, like all women and men born in the earth-bound state, know yourself as never-born, never knowable, never touched by the human blood and flesh. O Heaven born! Know your Heavenly Father and doubt not what He says.

Christ-Man: Am I Christ, who, some believe, would return?

God: God-Man! You are world's Saviour, who has returned to make a new world. Know yourself as the world's Words and believe that you are world's meaning as the incarnation of God. Christ is a power that emanates from God. You are world's force that has emanated from God. Christ is the matter-sprit-bound world's image of God who is not visible in form. Your image is the form through which the world may know and see Me. Christ is the moving world's matter-bound motion that suffers the destiny of life and death. You are moving as the matter-bound world's destiny and making yourself subject to life and death. Christ is moving as a power of Love and power to lift the world to God. You are world's force that is moving to make God's Love moving through the world and lifting the world to the Divine domain. Christ is the fallen state of the Divine incarnate as Man who is matter-spirit bound. Your fallen-state is where you exist in flesh and blood. Christ is moving and your formless state is moving as Christ in the world. Know you as Man-God, who is worldly and Divine. Christ as a historical man and a person is not what you are. Person has no meaning because God is no person of any race, creed or blood. Christ as Jesus is a false concept. Know God-Man as Christ, who is world's Saviour and the formless Work of God. Christ is you and you are Christ but not Jesus of Nazareth and you are one and the same. God is world's meaning and Christ is the meaning of the world. Christ is your worldly emanation from the void. Jesus is a man of flesh and blood while Christ is not.

Your Father has again moved to create you in human blood and flesh. Know the man in human blood and flesh as temporal and non-Christ, while you are Christ and the world's Saviour, who is God incarnate. Jesus is not who you are. Assume yourself not as what man is. Christ is not Man. Enter and exit where I am. Born of Heaven, who is not worldly, know you as Christ, who has returned. Both as Man and God you are Christ and the Poet, who is working in order to draw the men and the women towards world's Saviour, who is moving in the world to lift the world towards My Love.

Christ-Man: How do I relate to Buddha?

God: Buddha is a force that incarnates in the world as the moving matter-spirit-bound world's movement as reality. Buddha is the worldly manifestation of the will that is emanent in the world. Searching a meaning in the world, the mechanized state of life is moving as the controlling power that constitutes the matter-spirit world. Soul of Buddha is moving as the controlling mechanism that works to make the world exist. Assume yourself as the mechanized world's Saviour and emanate as the will that works to free itself from the mechanized destiny of the world. Both as Buddha and Christ you are world's movement in the wheel and outside the sentient world. God's movement as Buddha is the movement of the will that sees itself in the mechanized movements of the world. Both as Buddha and Christ you are the mechanized world's movement outside and inside the space and the time. Soul of Buddha is motion and motion is matter-bound. Buddha is moving and making the world emanent as will. Soul of man and woman are the soul of the worldly sorrowful Buddha moving as the will that works to free itself from the bondage of life and death tied to the wheel.

Christ-Man: Am I Buddha then?

God: Son! You are movement of the world's Saviour, who is moving to free the world from its destiny of life and death. God is working and through His work you are emanent in the world of will and form. Assume yourself as the moving and not-moving united as one. Buddha is a force that moves and creates the world in form. God's emanation is the movement of the world's will as Buddha emanating from the Lotus, that is the symbol of the world in form. Buddha "is" as the boundary of the form-giving sentient world beyond which there is no form. Buddha works as the world's motion and delusion where the sentient beings are destined to move while tied to the wheel of the mechanized world. Know yourself as the world's Saviour who is moving to free the sentient world from this form-giving will that is not free. Buddha is the boundary of the world where the void penetrates. Assume yourself as the world's formless void as well as the emanent world that penetrates the void. Assume the world as will and void as well as the matter-spirit bound mechanized world of motion, struggle and toil. Enter this world and move as matter-spirit bound existence and exit without moving in the motionless void. Assume the world as you and the worldly manifestation of Buddha. Doubt not your worldly existence as multiple motions of man and woman of the world. Both as Man and God you are multiple manifestations of One. Exotic existence of Buddha is moving as you and your will is manifest as Buddha in multiple forms. Bound to the matter-spirit world you are moving and making things move. The soul of Buddha is the world and the world is moving in the motion of matter where you are manifest in form. Son! God is. Enter the world as Buddha and return to the void. Entering you work; exiting you return and make no movement or work. God can not escape His own creation and there is nothing that can escape the realm of Buddha unless the existence dissolves in the void. Doubt not your existence confined in the void. Son! Buddha and Christ are the same. Christ is, and Buddha becomes. Christ moves; Buddha is transient and impermanent creating world's form. Christ is the movement of Man-God; Buddha is moving as sentient world willing to merge with the void. Both are moving and non-moving. Both are matter-spirit bound and the world and the no-world- i.e. the void. Both are world and will and work of the worldly will and the Divine power interconnected through form and void. Man-God! Doubt not the Words of God. Son! Doubt not the Words that emanate from the void.

Christ-Man: Who is the historic Buddha?

God: Doubt not your own existence as the historic Buddha. Once you are in form you are moving as a man of history. So was Buddha of the past. Know Buddha as the form giving aspect of existence. Therefore when you appear in form you are Buddha of form and the historic Buddha of the present. Assume not your body to be the same in all births. Being reborn you are world's exotic Buddha who appeared in the past. Assume Buddha to be the One and the same. Son! See yourself in the mirror of the world and doubt not your existence as the moving world's Buddha-to-be as well. The ego is governed by the worldly matter-spirit. Son! Surpass the ego and know yourself as the eternal and the same. Buddha as a sage, Buddha as a prince are conditioned thoughts. Surpass these conditioned concepts. Buddha is always the same. Son! Go and teach these to the women and the men. Doubt not the Words of your Father. Move!

The repentance: The causes of errors and follies

Christ-Man: If I have a Divine origin, I can not comprehend how I can be so weak, fallible, and bound to the instincts ? I have carried passion, desire, liking, disliking, fear, anxieties, despairs, hopes; I have felt enchanted by worldly success and depressed by failures. I have experienced despair while standing beside the stream of life and gazing at it without being able to stir and affect its motion. At the same time I have been afraid to plunge in the currents and eddies drawing life to its end. I have felt like a weak person, without any strength of the will and power to change the course, that moves against the way I have wished things to move. If I have descended from Heaven, tell me why have I lived such an existence? How shall I understand my role as the weak, fallible man who is driven by doubts, dilemmas and treacherous forces of thoughts that surge and disrupt the will to work and act to serve the Will of God?

God: Assume yourself as a man of the world, who carries the motions of the matter-spirit bound life enacted by the will that defines the life. But when you enter the domain, that is not governed by man, you are Me. Your daily life has not been any different from what a human life is, but your life is different from all in the domain where you are a part of God. Your life is an expression of what life represents as a moving will enacting the forces of life and death. God has willed your exist-

86

ence as a man because by being born as a man you will move the world towards God. God has willed your existence as a common human being because your will is not what a common human being will ever know without you yourself revealing God as a man. Enter the world and move as a man of desire, fear, anxiety, hate and love as the motion of the will that decides the life of man. Enter the world as motion of the matter-spirit-bound world and work for the Will that is beyond. God has willed the Work of God-Man as the motion of the will of man enacted by the Will of God, who has entered in the world in order to explain to man the working of God for man. Enter the worldly arena as a human being with desire and passion tied to the matter-bound cycles of life and death and make Me unveiled. God is working to make you work and let the world move towards Him. God has willed so, and therefore you can not will to make the world as will that permeates man's mind. What you will as a man is not what God has willed for man. Therefore remain attracted towards all that move and work to fulfil the meaning for which you are unveiled as God-Man. Enter the matter-spirit world and move, as you are moving, without repenting over your actions and let motivations of your actions be directed to the Will that is Divine. Both as a man and God you are working as will of man and not-working as the Will that is beyond. You are willing and not-willing. Your will is the formless movement of the world's Saviour. Know your weaknesses and fallibility as the motion of the world, and moving in the world make your life a movement of God-Man, who has entered the arena of life to work for the enlightenment of the world that moves in the matter-spirit-bound path. Enter the realm of man in order to move in the world of Man-God, who is "working" without working through the will of man. Your willing to be more than Man and decide over the human lot, as if you are the supreme power deciding over the man, is not what God is. Both as God-Man and Me you are world's meaning and salvation. Both as the world and the will you are form and void - the world and what lies beyond.

Christ-Man: If the Divine will is enacted through me and my will as a man is overridden by the will that works to make me move as Man-God, how shall I act in the world as a man? When the motive forces of the human will is operative in the blood and flesh, how shall I overcome the attractions of the will bound to the matter-spirit-world and act as a man, whose movements are willed by God? Tell me who am I that other human beings are not? Tell me what makes my existence the part of God while others are not God? Tell me amidst follies and errors of life how can I be beyond follies and errors of life? While my willing as a man is not what I am as God, tell me how am I existent with human will and how shall I know I am Man-God?

God: You are world's meaning and so make yourself the source of meaning that the world will understand. By being born and living in follies and errors of life you are moving in the world as Man-God, who has entered the world to make the errors and follies of life revealed as the acts of the human will and not as the Will of God. Both as Man and God your will and not-will are erroneous and not-erroneous. Both as will and not-will your world is folly and without folly. Both as will and not-will you are moving and not-moving. Son! Meaning of the world is what you are as God-Man, and not what you will as a man, who is willing to find meaning in the world as the matter-spirit-bound motion, that makes things appear in form. Know yourself as the moving error and folly that are above all errors and follies of the world and make yourself above the matter-spirit-bound world's movement creating erroneous impressions of the world that is immersed in the void. When you cross the boundary of the matter-spirit-world, there is no such concept of error and folly because what is God is God. Reality as you know, and that defines the concepts of errors and right and wrong, lies in the matter-spirit arena where man can not know what is outside and how to move in the domain that is beyond. God has willed your existence in order to make man move in the domain of God. Both as Man and God your world is the world of matter-spirit and the domain that is not existing in the sense of existence that man conceive. Man-God! You are the meaning of the world and make your manifestation in the world the meaning of the will that moves the world in the realm of Man-God. Know that you are all and none. Know yourself as all - when you are manifest as the will of man , and none - when you are moving as the matter-spirit-bound world's Saviour and My Son. Son! Sorrow, desire, worldly ambitions are all created by the will that is willing to abandon the world of form. Therefore work to make man's will move beyond the world of sorrow, desire and ambitions driven by power, greed and lust.

Christ-Man: If the renunciation of the will to dominate, consume and live at the expense of others should be the enlightened way, why then the human will is empowered with the force that wills-to-power and wills-to-consume the world with passion and lust? What causes this error? Why must man live life that leads to such treacherous paths? Why have I been unable to control the forces of the will that drags man to the instinctual path? When things are as they are why shall man aspire to move beyond what is given as the reality? Why shall man seek God? Why have you thrown the will to live and struggle in the world in such calamitous path? How does it matter for human beings, if they know God's mystery or not? What is the meaning of salvation when life must exist in the matter-bound state and move forever in the wheel of life and death? By knowing about the world that is beyond, what shall man know? If one abandons the enlightened path in which way will he or she suffer more than what all life will suffer as a result of birth?

God: God-Man! Reality is a path that is directed by the will that keeps the matter-spirit world bound. As a worldly man every human existence is bound to experience this drag of the will controlling the reality of the world. Both as man and part of God human existence must refer to Man-God and man must know that the reality is only one aspect of the existence to which all life belong. Both as Man and God the existence of Man-God is all and none. In all He is existent as Man-God, though He is none. As world's Saviour tell man about your nature and the way the life is sustained and destroyed. By gaining this knowledge man will know the movement of God as Man in the world who is existent in form. By the process of searching beyond, man can know the reality that is deeper than the matter-spirit world and realize the meaning of life in the Saviour, who has incarnated to make man free. World was, is and will be and the matter-spirit world will create and destroy what will is meant to create and destroy. Bondage to this reality is the matter-bound soul's destiny that no life will be able to bypass. However, when the life moves by the force of the will governing the instincts alone, it decays and life's bondage to the matter-bound state increases. Boundary of the matter-spirit world defines the boundary beyond which life has another dimension. Once the human mind is enlightened about this path that leads to the domain beyond, the human life can realize the higher-domain of existence in the realm of Man-God. The reality will appear different once man will be able to see the domain that exists beyond. Knowing one's relation with Man-God, human life will be willing to explore the movement of Man-God within themselves as the movement of God. By knowing about the domain that is beyond they will know the matter-spirit-bound world's boundary and the realm of God, where the matter-bound life can not enter and where God is the force of Love. In suffering and error they will be able to see the hands of God as the matter-bound world's Saviour, who is attracting all towards Him. The instinctual desire may be eliminated once man knows the way of Man-God. The instincts are moving in the world in order to bind the man in the world of form. God-Man is creating the force to make man move outside this realm of form. The boundary of one is coupled to the boundary of the other in the matter-spirit state working together to create the world as the soul and the body. Boundary of the soul is formless while the body has form. Realizing the movement of the formless in form one can free oneself from the destiny-bound world where the will moves. Thus one cane see the realm of God revealed through Man-God. By creating the world the will is set free and the matter is bound in laws. Both are united in the realm of matter-spirit that creates and destroys the world through the movements of the will and form. The role of God is not to move with the world as manifest in the will and form. God-Man is the moving force that establishes the link between the matter-spirit world and the domain of God. Though bound, man can know his relation to God through God-Man and become free from the matter-spirit-world by moving with Him. Thus there exists the path of salvation and knowing God man may know himself as a part of the World's Saviour who is moving and working as God incarnate. How does this knowledge help? You may ask. Know that the world is and is-not. What you see and wish to know about is and is-not. God has willed so and to see God's mystery unveiled you should know the enlightened path. Know your sorrow, desire, love, hate, despair etc. as the illusion of the matter-spirit-world where will is manifest. Once man knows the enlightened way such follies of the mind will disappear and man will see God's Love drawing man to the Divine path. By abandoning the enlightened way man will follow the bondage and the movements of the forces that draw existence from the formless to the matter-bound state, that creates the sufferings and illusions of the world. How does it matter, if man suffers or not? You may wonder. How do you know what is not-suffering and how shall man decide if suffering is to be abandoned for not-suffering? Know that suffering is a state of the will that draws and destroys while not suffering is a state that creates no motion or thought. The suffering is a power to make the world and attract it towards the state of not-suffering. Both suffering and not-suffering must exist so that the world may be revealed as the Work of God. Holding to suffering's path without seeking salvation's way will lead to destruction and chaos. Suffering works to end in not-suffering and therefore freedom of the soul can not escape the attraction of the Love of God. Know this working mechanism of the Divine Love and make man move along the enlightened path.

Renunciation of the instinctual pleasure. The way that illumines

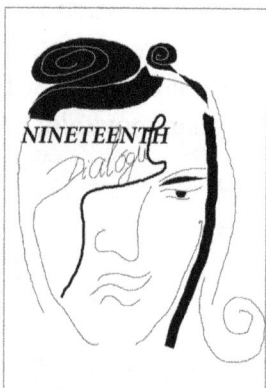

Christ-Man: What creates sexuality? Why sexual drives arise mostly at night? Should man abandon sexuality and avoid the life that brings sexual urges? Why sexuality has an overwhelming power over the body and creates the senses of pleasures?

God: Sexuality is a power to keep human life engaged in reproducing itself from the matter-spirit-world and making oneself bound to the matter-spirit-forces that drive the wheel of life and death. The sexual urges are conditioned by the will that creates and destroys. Bound to life, the will is set to move to create the sexual urges so that matter-spirit world can sustain the process of recreating itself and make everything matter-spirit bound. The sexuality is moving in order to make man fall in the domain where life is moving to accomplish the matter-spirit-bound world's unsurpassable fate. But the world has more movements than the movement of the destiny-bound sexual life of women and men. The world can exist without the reproduction of the matter-spirit world and this world has no form. Working in the domain, that is sexually bound, man will not be able to move beyond the world of the form and the will that sustains the power of destiny. Working as men and women, who are sexually bound in order to create the world, men and women work for the forces that bind life to instincts, desires and lust. For man and woman there exist other paths. The matter-bound world is a prison of the dark forces that create and destroy. Knowing this, woman and man should seek to avoid the path where the sexuality is working and they should search the path of Man-God. The will, that is set to make man seek sexual relation, is the will to live and captivate the world in the matter-spirit-bound movement. Knowing this worldly will, that makes man and woman work for the sexual life, move beyond the world and know the domain that is immersed in the Eternal Light. Knowing the matter-spirit-bound world's fate avoid the destiny that makes man fall in the matter-bound state. Knowing that the state of life moves in many more worlds than the world where sex operates, work to free human life from the bondage of life and death. Knowing the world as an illusion work for the world that is beyond illusion. Knowing that the world is and is-not, work for Man-God, who attracts the world towards the domain that lies beyond. God has created man and woman to work and move in the matter-spirit-bound existence. Know that this existence of man and woman has many dimensions beyond the sexual life. The pleasure, that is sexual and makes man destined to live in the matter-spirit-bound world, is the pleasure that creates the instincts that bind the world in the darkened state. The body exhilarates because the body is the source of pleasure, where will implants itself as the power of fate. Knowing the working of the body and the will, from which the body derives pleasure and remains engaged in the process of life and death, work for the worldly life's movement and be attracted by Man-God, who shows man the way outside the bondage of life and death.

Christ-Man: If man and woman should avoid sexual life how shall life continue?

God: God has willed that man and woman should be attracted in order to create the world; but the world, that is seen, felt or touched, is not all that exist. Knowing the world that lies beyond, man and woman should seek the world that is moving to make life one with God. How does it work when man and woman must remain attracted towards each other in sexual life? Know that by willing to make the world as matter and will God has made Himself separate from the existence, that remains united with God through the existence of God-Man. God-Man

93

is moving to unite man with God. Knowing His love and loving Him as God, who moves in the world, remain engaged in the matter-spirit-bound world. Son! God is no-will of man, but through the will that He has created, God has assumed the worldly existence of God-Man. How shall man avoid sexual life and move through the matter-spirit world when the life should move and can not come to a halt? Knowing that the sexual desires are working to make what life must, leave the matter-bound world's movement and seek unity with God. God has created man and woman to experience His Love. But by loving the body, man and woman only love the will that is not the true source of His Love. Knowing the Love that attracts the world and makes it move beyond the domain, where life is bound, man and woman should move to the source of Love, that moves outside the boundary of the bodily passion and pleasure. Without the attraction of the sexes, and the pleasures of the body, Love will cease to exist in the bodily form, but love is more than the sexual world. Enter the arena where God has created God-Man and know the Light that emanates from Him. How does this Love can free man when life must continue? How does it free man when freedom is in bondage in the world? God has made God-Man to relate this freedom with the bondage. Enter in the life and remain engaged as man and woman seeking Love and desiring to be free. Freedom is not a state where man is free from the instinctual world but a freedom where man can escape the instinctual world's force and move beyond the world, where God is and is-not. Moving towards Him, man and woman will be free from the instinctual world's fate-bound state. How? You man ask. Know that, bound to the soul and the will, world is fate-bound. But when they do not make the reality of the sensual world as the sole meaning and purpose of life man and woman can move outside this fate-bound existence. Both as Man and God, Man-God is matter-spirit bound and at the same time free. Knowing Him as the Saviour, when the world moves towards Him, man and woman will not desire for desiring the bodily pleasure but will move to make human life an expression of His Love, that is free and moves to make the world one with Him. How does it work when desire must exist in order to create the world bound in body and form? How does it relate when relating to the body is a source of desire that makes man bound? How does it work when Love is not what desire is? God has created

God-Man to unite these opposites as one. Knowing His working in the world, man and woman will know that God is and is-not. Man-God your world is and is-not. Knowing you as existent and non-existent at the same time man and woman will know the meaning of human desire and Godly Love. Knowing you as working and not-working as the will, that is bound and at the same time free, the world will move to create what is and rest in what is-not: What is in God and what appears as separate from Him.

Christ-Man: If the world is self-contained, when man falls to the sense-bound state or moves towards the bodily existence what is the meaning of right and wrong? Why the bodily pleasure should be called the darkness and the renunciation of the sexual desires and the worldly will be considered as the light that illumines?

God: Bound to the matter-spirit-world the desire that creates illusions and makes man see the world as the one that is sense-bound is the source of confinement of the mind. In this state man is unable to see what is beyond. It is darkness because the world is limited by the sense bound signals and the will that sees and interprets the world according to the movements of the matter-bound state. The soul is not able to relate itself with the greater domains of existence. So the world is governed by a will that make everything bound to the matter-world. But when the domain of the senses are crossed, the world appears with its many dimensions. The world "appears" as is and is-not. Both in and outside "appear" as the moving world and the non-moving sphere – one is ephemeral and other is eternal. Both the world that appears and the world that "appears not", are united. Both as related to God and separate from God the world and the will "appear" with its multitude of motions. Beyond the boundary of the senses the world takes innumerable shapes and forms. Entering this state one sees depths of the mind and innumerable worlds, that are worlds within worlds...moving ad infinitum without any end. In this state one thus realizes the limitations of the matter-bound sensory world and "sees" the infinite. The world appears as being revealed by an inner Light. Enter this Light and know this greater state of existence that is Divine.

Matter, mind, brain. God and void

Christ-Man: You have talked about the Light, the vision of the infinite, the experience of the Divine world as something that transcends all joys and visions, that can be experienced and seen in the world, but I experience no ecstasy and joy. I only hear the words that emanate from You and experience the waves that move in the inner domain without moving in the world. Through these Words the visions are excited as pure thoughts, where there is no light, no sound or signal to excite the physical body the way the body enjoys pleasure and joy. It is like a dream...not one but innumerable ones convoluted inside each other ...going deeper and deeper in the domain where there is no sound, vision, and experience of the body. This world is empty and nothing, that is submerged in greater and greater emptiness, that thoughts can not reach. In this emptiness, I hear Your voice. Nothing else seem to exist in this world except the coiling energy that surges and penetrates the mind in order to make me work and move. The light, the vision, the excitements of seeing something beautiful seem to pertain to the world where the body is sense-bound. In the Divine world the mind penetrates the domains where the inner forces distort everything seen, heard and experienced by the senses. It projects the world as a collection of surreal dreams, that penetrate each other, and float in an infinite void. Through the movements of this surreal, that penetrates the real, I know that there exists the "Divine world", that I can not see, feel or touch. I do not know how this happens. Is it a process triggered in the brain? Who triggers it? How is it triggered? I have no way to know. How shall I know that what I experience as the Divine are not phenomena in the brain, that is activating the cells from the dormant states and thus self-activating the illusion of the movements of the waves, from which the words seem to emanate? Tell me, how shall I understand and decide what is true and false? How shall I enjoy this vision of the eternal Light when there is no light at all?

God: Assume that the mind is a phenomenon, that is outside the matter-bound state. Knowing the mind as outside matter and something that is moving in the matter-world, you should understand the words as the words that emanate from the mind, that moves and makes you hear the voice of God. Assume not the words as the phenomenon of the brain. The brain is not able to activate the cells the way the mind is able to activate the brain. Both as mind, and the brain activated by the mind, the voice appears to the mind as a movement of the energy that makes no motion in the material sphere. I am not any energy of the material domain but an "energy" that makes matter move and create energy of the world. God's force is not what forces matter to move, but that creates the movement of the soul to make mind activate the brain and relate itself to the material domain. God's force has no counter-part in the matter world and therefore it can become a-causal and a-temporal, as if time and space has no meaning in the realm of God. God's force is making your mind move in the temporal world and this movement is causing the words to appear as movements of thoughts. God has no relation to the mind, which appears as matter-bound world's phenomenon of the brain. God is and is-not. Brain moves according to the matter-bound principles of action. Brain is not what makes mind move. Mind is a phenomenon of the a-causal world that activates the movement of the cells and awaken the brain to move and relate the physical components of the body according to causal relationship of the world. Assume this process to be true. Both as mind and matter, the movements of the world and the will are making man and woman conscious of the world as matter and mind. God is, however, not a part of this scheme. Assume Him as the words that emanate and impinge on the mind that generates the actions to move the matter-bound brain to conceive that what is beyond. Assuming that the brain is the power that can generate the words as self-activating illusory process, is a false concept of what mind and the Words are. Bound to the world the mind is moving as a self-realizing process, that couples the matter with the mind. Without this unity the words will remain unknown to the mind. Both as matter and mind the process is not self-conflicting but self-illuminating. Bound to the world, this self-illuminating movement is the source of all words that can not be grasped by the process of the mind that is not illumined. Bound to this process, working in the mind, your words are moving as the illumination of God.

THE FOLLOWING DIALOGUES ARE ABOUT THE WAY THE CHRIST-MAN IS ABLE TO LEAVE THE DIVINE REALM AND COME DOWN TO THE SPHERE OF MAN IN FLESH AND BLOOD, WHERE EGO AND WILL RULE THE MOVEMENTS AND ACTIVITIES OF LIFE. THE DIALOGUES ALSO INCLUDE THE WAY HE MAY AGAIN RETURN BACK TO GOD AFTER HIS MISSION IN LIFE ON EARTH IS COMPLETE.

Part II

THE RIGHT WAY TO GO DOWN AND RETURN

The preparation before going down

Christ-Man: Before I go down, tell me what path shall I choose and what mask shall I wear? How shall I prepare myself for the encounter with women and men?

God: Born of woman and man, your physical appearance will be indistinguishable from other women and men. Entering the world you should make yourself indistinguishable from women and men while you encounter them. Both as Man and God, you must move as Man and work for the will that has created you as the messenger of God. God will move with you. Prepare yourself for the matter-spirit world's destiny that may affect your physical condition. Working amidst women and men, O Heaven born! you will work for the matter-spirit world's meaning and the common man's way to find this mountain way. Knowing your Godly birth, know that you are free from all sin and knowing that sin is not anything that pertains to Man-God, you should perform the work that men and the women will perform as sinful acts. Working and performing the daily tasks as a common man you should bring yourself close to the common women and men. Knowing yourself as the world's Saviour you should know that the world is God's love and the world is saved by Man-God moving in the worldly arena as God incarnate. Knowing yourself as

Man-God, know that God has willed your existence in order to show women and men the enlightened path.

Christ-Man: Knowing myself as someone born of Heaven how shall make myself unknown to the women and men? And why shall I not tell them who I am?

God: Knowing your worldly manifestation as Man, you will move as Man-God united as one. Both as Man and God you will be in the world but do not seek from women and men their worldly understanding of God and Man. They will not understand what you will be saying and may make your working in the world difficult to perform. Without knowing you as Me, they will assume you as a worldly man. Knowing you as a worldly man they will know the movement of Man-God. Knowing you as God they will not understand that man is not God. Both as Man and God how shall you explain that you are neither man nor God but a man who is God incarnate? O Heaven born! The world is awaiting for your down coming. Go down and show the women and th men the path to the world from where you have come.

Christ-Man: The paths, that move downwards, are full of danger and distress. O Father of Heaven! How shall I go down knowing the sufferings on the way? In sin how shall I remain sinless? In living with men and women, who suffer from hunger and thirst, greed and lust, and exhilarate or feel distress over love and hate, how shall I remain aloof and at the same time remain engaged in the world, where men and women work and strive for fame, honour, power and fulfill the instinctual necessities driving the activities of the days?

God: Enter the world as if you are nothing but one of them. Knowing yourself as the moving God, who has come to the world to make man move to the enlightened way, work and move in the down-fallen state. Know the women and the men as your parts. Knowing their desires and lusts work so that they can know the greater path. Go the way all human beings are going downward under the darkened vault and make yourself the world's meaning by moving as Man-God among them. Go the way the women and the men are searching fame, honour and seeking to control the forces that dominate over the matter and exposed to the dangers of the matter-spirit bound fate. Free the women and the men from the ignorance that have darkened their ways. Knowing yourself as God-Man, know that no sin can touch you and no matter-spirit bound destiny can draw you to dangers of the fate-bound life of the women and the men. You are Bound and Free. Son! Work for the freedom of the world that is bound. Assume yourself as world and will and no-world and no-will and move as the world and will and no-world and no-will. Born of Heaven, you are working and moving in order to make men and women move towards the world where nothing work or move. Son! The world is awaiting your down-coming. Go and move along the darkened path. I shall move with you and guide you through the sufferings that cover the human world. Born of Heaven, you are the Light of Heaven that will illumine Earth. Bound and free, go and move as God's Light! Enter the suffering world and make the world know about the Light from where you have come.

The right way to find the enlightened path

Christ-Man: I am afraid, when I shall descend in that darkened valley, I may not find my way back to the height where we meet. Tell me, after I have finished the task, how shall I find the way to return.

God: The woman and man, bound to the world, will not be able to find this way. Bound to the world they have to know My Son and the way He asks them to go. Born of man and woman your form is human but your soul is not of a man. Your way is not the way any man can walk with the behest of the will that makes man move. Your words will make them moving towards your worldly path, where they will meet Man-God as God and Man united in the world of will with no-world and no-will. You are not one of them and your world is not darkened by the will that darkens the souls. Bound and free, you will see the Light that emanates from Me. Born of man and woman your worldly existence will move as Man and your Divine counterpart will show you where and how to move. Your fear of not being able to find the way is the fear that arises from the mind still enshrouded with ignorance. Son! Work and move! See the world as darkened by the will, and see Me amidst that darkness as the Light of God.

Christ-Man: If no man can walk long the way I shall return which path shall I show?

God: Knowing your incarnation as Man-God, man and woman will know the path where they should walk. Knowing your words as the Words of God, they will move in the world as the parts of Man-God, who are bound and free in the domain of the earthly and the Divine. Knowing the man and the woman as your parts know the movement of yourself through the world as woman and man, whose paths are darkened by the will and the world and lightened by the world's Saviour walking with them. Tell them that the world is not governed by the matter alone but it is a work of the will that works-not and wills-not the way all existence are bound in the world and the will. Tell them that their salvation lies in the path that has been paved by Man-God in being born and incarnated as a man of blood and flesh. Entering the world you have worked for the salvation of the world and brought meaning of the human life, where worldly and Divine are united as Man-God. God is the world's Saviour and by sending His Son to the world He has made life meaningful. Know the meaning in being one with the Will of God - will and world and no-will and no-world bound through Man-God. Knowing you as Me and the world as the manifestation of God as world's Saviour, who is working to make all move towards Him through God-Man, man and woman will see what is beyond and what illumines. Knowing this formless source of illumination, that sees the world from the height where we are, the women and men will be able to see what can not be seen. Knowing this, Son! work and see yourself in the mirror of the world as the Divine light that illumines the darkness that covers the world.

Christ-Man: How shall man cleanse the soul and purify the mind in order to see Thy mystery unveiled? O Father of Heaven! How shall they know your Love amidst sorrow and grief, while the instincts bring the pleasure of bodily birth, what shall make them abandon the instinctual way, and in which way shall I help them see, that can not be seen, while the reality of the world - as seen and known - persuades them to act and think differently?

God: Born of man and woman they do not know what works behind the forces of life and death. Bound to the instincts and the forces appearing as the will they are working to serve the matter-bound world's fate. Son! God is working where Man-God is emanent from Heaven as a link to the world. God's working is not known to the matter-spirit bound life and therefore the will, driving the instincts, are moving as the powerful mechanism to form and shape. Once the world knows what is moving beyond all movements, the woman and man will work for what is not bound to the will of man. Son! To make them see that can not be seen is the reason why you are. By seeing you as a man and knowing you as God they will realize the movement of the world's Saviour working to make man free from the instinctual life and lift them towards the Love of God. Knowing the working of Man-God, they will work for the liberation of man and woman, who are bound to the will and form. God is not what they may think about God. God is not what they want to know about God. God is not what they wish to make of God and want Him to be! God is what is in all and nothing that can be conceived. Assume yourself as Him and propagate the Words that emanate from Him. How will the world move and follow the path of the world's Saviour, when the world can not see God, is why God-Man has entered the world. Move as Him. Road to Me is not the worldly road to move. To see Me unveiled woman and man should move along the path that Son of God has paved.

Christ-Man: What preparation of the mind is needed to see Thy Light unveiled?

God: Son! What moves is moving, and what does not move is making all movements emanent from the source from where you hear the Words. God wills not the way the will of the human beings function. There is no meaning in willing to see the mystery of God unveiled or not. Such willing is a projection of the worldly understanding of what are available to thoughts. Knowing the work of Man-God and the way the world is projected through Him as a part of Man and God, willing to see God will reveal Man-God, as the movement of the Words. Man can only know Me through the words of Man-God. Doubt not your power to see beyond and make the world move towards the domain where you see My Mystery unveiled. Only through the Words, that I reveal through you, the world will be able to conceive the mystery, that is God. How shall man and woman prepare themselves for the Divine encounter? Knowing the world as God revealed through His Son, the woman and the man should move to the road where I am world's Saviour moving in the world to make man free. Knowing Me as Man-God, the world will encounter the Divine as the Words that work to make man free from the world's bondage. Your movement in the world is working to prepare them to the journey on the road where man will encounter the mystery of the Divine. Know Me unveiled as you and your words will prepare them for an encounter that will lead man and woman seek the higher way.

Right concepts and visions

Christ-Man: What shall I teach to the women and the men? What are the right concepts of the world, man and God so that they may understand these Words of God ?

God: How do you teach? The words are methods by which man and woman build concepts of the world, man, and God. Born as woman and man they can not understand what is beyond the sensory world and what can not be seen. What Man-God will teach will be the foundation on which they should build the concepts of the world, man, and God. Man-God is a phenomenon that is world's mystery and can not be conceived by human thoughts. Born of flesh and blood your existence, that pertains to the world, is what man and woman will be able to conceive. Entering the world you will make them see what can not be seen. Son! What is concept? What makes the world and the will move without the working of the force that makes man conceive? Knowing that conceiving is not-conceiving, and conceiving the world as the matter-bound form is not-conceiving the nature of the world, man and woman will conceive what can not be conceived. Assume yourself as the foundation of the concepts that move and will make the world conceive what man, God and nature are. What more they can conceive when all concepts are no-concepts, when bound to the matter-bound thoughts? By conceiving the world as sense-given data of causal meaning and relations they will misconceive what real is, and what makes reality felt and seen. Bound to the matter-spirit, the world is a plethora of concepts, that need to be developed as one works and moves in the matter-spirit domain. Like looking in multiple mirrors moving with respect to the objects, the will develops its own projection and image in the world and sees itself through innumerable concepts. Bound to the causal world there is no one concept that will make man understand the reality of the world, man and God. Born of man and woman they are accustomed to conceive the world through the limited understandings of what has been seen, and heard. God can not be conceived through such limited knowledge and understanding. Man-God is working to make them conceive that the world is and is-not. Both as existing and non-existing the world is and is-not. Both as world and will and no-world and no-will the existence is and is-not. God is and is-not. Entering and working in the world Man-God is the foundation on which the existence can move in the causal arena of will and world that interpenetrate and interact with each other to form concepts. Boundary of this world, that is conceivable by the sensory data, is limited to the mechanisms that work only in the arena where the matter-spirit move and interact. This boundary of the world is and is-not. Bound to the mind, wich sees the boundary, the world is, and when free from the constraints of the causal movements the world is-not. The world appears as "is", when it is conceived through concepts that are reflections of the mind that sees itself in the moving world, where matter-spirit are working. The world is-not when the cessation of the matter-spirit movements cause the will and the world to disappear and the world becomes one with the unmoved. This matter-spirit is the source of the world and will. Son! Work for the cessation of this movement and let man and woman move towards the unmoved.

Christ-Man: What is the right vision? Which vision of God should man keep in mind when they search the domain of the Divine?

God: God is and is-not. Both as the world and the will, that is matter-spirit bound, God manifests in the world as Man-God and moves as the world's Saviour to make man free from the world's bondage. God is-not, when the world is seen as the mind from which all emanate. Voice of God is the only reality that can penetrate the realm of the world and the will, that move in the matter-spirit bound state. God-Man is the world's Saviour who hears and transmits these words to the world. Bound to the human existence, the man and woman can not know anything beyond what is said of God by His Son. Knowing Him as God-Man, man and woman will know Me as the world and the will and no-world and no-will co-existent in the reality of the world that is also beyond what is called the reality by the sense-bound concepts. Knowing Him as Me and the world's Saviour, who moves in the world to free man from the worldly bondage, the woman and man should visualize My Godly existence as a force that emanates from the void. He is and is-not. God can not be understood and no visual method can help to comprehend what and who is He? The Words of God-Man is the only method to make man see what is not seen. The words bring matter-bound concepts. But there is no method to make the words devoid of the concepts that relate to the sense-bound world. Whatever way the words can be said they will always move in the imaginary world, that can not express who God is. Vision of God as Man and a person is only a vision in the matter-bound world where the mind looks at itself in the mirrors of the moving world. Entering the world your worldly incarnation has experienced the matter-bound world's movement and your words are being formed through the matter-spirit-bound world's experience. Assume these words to be emanating from a source, that is God. How do you see Him? How do you conceive which is-not? How do you work and live with Him when you are fate-bound world's movement as Man-God? God-Man! You are the source of the world and the will that the man and the woman should keep in mind while seeking the liberation from the world. Son! Your physical image is not what they should imagine as God, but imagining God through you they should see Christ in themselves. Go and teach man about this enlightened way.

Right thoughts in relation to nature, and life

Christ-Man: What shall be the right thoughts when man must live in nature and live by consuming plants and animals that they need to kill and destroy?

God: Born of man and woman, human life is dependent on the matter and the spiritual encounter with the moving world. Knowing the necessity of the existence as destined by the matter-spirit bound fate, man and woman should make themselves parts of the nature and work to fulfil the moving world's destiny as world and will which act and react back, so that the wheel of life and death can move. Knowing the world as the powerful manifestation of the will, that has created the world, man and woman should act in faith to the matter-spirit world's Saviour and know themselves as parts of the same that eat and destroy and compose and create. Knowing the matter-spirit bound world and the will striving to move outside the arena of the world and the will, man and woman must work and act as destined by fate. Knowing the world and the will as movements that have to be continued in order to make the process of life and death renewing the world at every turn of the wheel, man and woman should think of themselves as the world and will united in the body of flesh. In entering the world and will man and woman have sacrificed themselves to the moving wheel that composes and creates and kills and destroys. Knowing the destiny, that assumes that the world and will to move according to the matter-spirit bound world's fate, woman and man should relate to the moving wheel as the world and the will incarnate in human flesh. Knowing the world and will as the work of God, man and woman should make themselves attracted and destroyed in order to bring forth new life. Knowing the world and the will where God is and is-not, woman and man should work for what are, and develop insight into the matter-spirit world's movement of fate. God is and is -not, and being the creation of God, man and woman should know that there is nothing that is killed and destroyed. What appears as life is what is and is-not. What appears as death, is and is-not. God is and is-not in both life and death. Knowing Him as the world's Saviour enter the sacrifice in the wheel.

Christ-Man: What purpose and meaning this sacrifice have?

God: God is and is-not. What meaning is, when God has willed so and what purpose means when God has willed the world and will to exist? The purpose is to exist and renew the world so that nothing remains what it was. The meaning in the renewal lies in the working of God in making things appear in the matter-spirit world through the will that contradicts and moves in order to destroy and create. Without the contradictions nothing would exist and without existence there will be nothing that will move and appear.

Christ-Man: Why everything is not God, void and tranquillity? Why did you create the moving world that never ceases, never remains the same, never brings resolution of the conflicts and struggles among all that exist in forms? Why things must disappear and reappear anew?

God: Bound to the existence as world and will God is and is-not. What is "is" is-not, and what is "is-not" is "is". Entering the world and will God has made Himself appear as the world and the will. Bound to the world and the will this appearance has made all to move and disappear. Both as appearing in the world and the will, and disappearing in the void I am emanent and transcendent in form and as formless. Through creation I am emanent in the world and will and through disappearance, where there is no world and will, I am transcendent. How do you exist beyond the will and the world if the will and the world are the only essence that exist? How do you remain in Me as well as outside where everything is tranquil? How do you work when there is no-working in the realm where I am? How do you move when movements are matter-bound? Both as world and will and no-world and no-will I am, and the world exists where God-Man is incarnate. The world and the will can be transcended by the power of the will that moves in the world. Knowing this power lies in man and woman themselves, the world can escape the wheel of life and death and enter the void. The meaning of existence is to move towards this state and be one with the void where there is no-existence of the world and the will, that cretae all. How do you enter this state when everything are motions and full of contradictions? How do you know that there exist what can not be expressed as something existing? Knowing Me as tranquil and void, enter the world and will and work to fulfil the state of existence where I am emanent.

Christ-Man: What create sorrow and suffering?

God: Know yourself as Man-God, who is God incarnate in flesh and blood. Knowing yourself as Me know the unity of all. Knowing the unity, work to free man from the bondage of life and death. Knowing the world and the will, fated to move and exist in contradictions and struggle, know the meaning of the working of God. When the human beings will develop the understanding of the Words of God, they will grieve not and suffer not in confronting what is the fate of all. What creates suffering? If I cease to move in the world the contradictions will disappear and all movements will cease. Will this be an end to what you call suffering? By existing there exist the contradictions and through contradictions one knows the world and the will that move, and through these movements the world and the will strive to reach what is beyond. This is the way to move.

Christ-Man: If everything is fated to be destroyed why do You ask me to show compassion to life and revere it with love?

God: Your compassion is not for the life and death that must work in order to make the world and the will to exist. Knowing the world as your parts your will is working to attract all to yourself by using the power of Love. The compassion and Love are what make you the source of the power with which you draw the beings towards yourself. Once in motion towards you, they move in the conflict torn arena of the world and the will and Love makes the world the moving power that destroys what is, and renews.

Christ-Man: Why do you work in my heart as a source of Love, that teaches man not to kill and destroy?

God: Your life as a man of flesh and blood is Godly and knowing God's Love your mind is suffused with compassion and Love for all. When killing and destruction appear you remember the meaning of God's Love to lift the world towards Him. He is moving in the world in order to free man from the bondage of life and death. Knowing yourself as Him, in your down-fallen human state you will not to destroy, what belongs to God. God is formless movement in the hearts of all, and by destroying what is, you destroy yourself. God is working within you in order to create the force that attracts in order to bring human life to a higher state. Both as the destroyer of life and the world's Saviour, who works to make things move towards Him, God has implanted in you the will to Love although things are fated to be destroyed. By loving you create the power that moves all to God and by moving towards God all are released from the matter-spirit bound fate. Killing and destruction powered by the will, that does not see the loving hands of God, and makes the world instinct bound, serve no higher purpose than turning the wheel of life and death. Bound to the wheel, man and woman, should strive to move beyond the world and the will. And the way to move beyond is the way of love and reverence for what are created by God. God's working is not the same as the working of the will of man and God's movement is not the same as the movements of the will and the world. Knowing your incarnation as God-Man, love what is, and love-not what is not willed by God. Son! The world is waiting for your down-coming. Go down and move as My Love.

The will and the individual

Christ-Man: Man and woman are born before they know that they have been born. Their births are not dependent on whether they will to be born or not. They find themselves in the life's arena. Once born, they must choose and make use of the will that they inherit on birth and remain engaged in the struggles and contradictions of life and death. How shall man look at his or her life and take the responsibility for the will they inherit, whie originally they are not responsible for receiving this will. If the will, that they carry, is the result and consequence of the actions of the other human beings and their will, who have given them births, how shall man understand one's role in life's arena and take responsibility for the will that makes them choose and act?

God: Born as woman and man human beings must remain in the world and will and move as destined by the matter-spirit-bound fate. Willing not to be born has no meaning because will is not separate from what is not born and born. The will and the world are attracted and destroyed by the movements of the matter-spirit-bound fate. God has willed so and not willing to be born has no meaning in a world where will of God is moving as the will of all. Born as a woman and a man, man must will and act. Both in willing and not-willing to act, the human will remains moving through the world as the matter-spirit bound world's destiny, that no man and woman can surpass by the will that they wish to employ in escaping the wheel of death and birth. Will of the one, that gives birth of the another, is the will that is destined to remain the will of the world and therefore no-willing to move in the world and will, as a man of human birth, has no meaning in the world. The life must move with death and through life and death the will shall remain in the world as the moving power that upholds the world. The will of the one, who is born, is not that never remained before. The one, who is born, is a will that manifests through what was and what remained as the will of the world before some one took his or her place in life's arena amidst struggles and contradictions. Will is not separate from what are born and unborn. The birth is a manifestation of the will through form. Therefore in form the will appears visible to itself in the matter-spirit-bound world, and moves to fulfill the destiny for which the will exists in the world. Born as a man and woman is not to be born as a will that is separate from those that once were born before. Once born, the will remains in the world and carries itself through the process of contradictions and moves. Carrying the will to the world through the matter-bound state the existence becomes emanent in form, while the non-existence remains unknown to the existence that becomes. Knowing this, man and woman should act as the will that remains in the world as the destiny of the matter-bound world and know that willing of man and woman is willed before they exist in form. Bound to the world and the will, work and remain engaged as a man or a woman, who are moving in the world as the movements of Man-God. Women and men should move as if they are parts of Man-God, who is willing in the world of flesh and blood as Man and not-willing as God.

Christ-Man: What meaning the will of an individual has? How shall man understand the meaning of what one wills and wills-not? Why human existence appears as the conflicts of the will among the individuals, and if there is no such individual will, how shall man understand these conflicts?

God: Assume the individuals as the manifestation of the One in many physical states. Being born in the physical state the will sees itself in the physical condition in which the existence appears. Bound to the laws of the matter and the necessities of the movements, that make the world incessantly struggling against the matter-spirit-bound fate, the individual consciousness appears in the world. Through this consciousness, man and woman see the limitations of the physical and mental realms. Both as the will, that is not separate from the world and others, and the conditioned thoughts, that separate the physical entities from the other physical entities, man and woman become conscious of themselves as individuals, who work against the needs and necessities of the others for the benefits of their own. Born in the matter-spirit-bound arena, the will is thus working to make itself moving against itself in order to resolve the contradictions that make everything move. God has willed so and therefore man should remain engaged in the struggles and contradictions and strive to move outside the area of the matter-spirit-bound fate.

Christ-Man: How can man know that will is one and individuals are not separate from the Will that makes all move?

God: Will is world and world is will. Knowing the world as the manifestation of the will, that seeks to move outside the matter-spirit-bound domain, woman and man should know about the movements of the world in the will, that remains in the world although the forms and shapes may disappear from the sensory states. Knowing the movement of the force that makes all attracted towards itself, the matter-bound world's movement should be seen as the movement of the world as willed by the force, that makes all bound to existence in forms. God is and is-not. God is in the world as the moving world's will, that attracts and creates the movements that separate the objects from each other by setting them in contradictions and conflicts; God is-not in the world as the world's Saviour, who is willing-not to move as the world and the will and making the world disappear towards Him. How do you understand this dichotomy between what is and is-not? How do you know what "is" is "is-not"? Knowing the world and the will as the arena where Man-God is manifest, will and will-not the way the life separates from itself, and works to fulfil the movement of fate. Make yourself the Saviour of the world, who has appeared in flesh and blood in order to lead man and woman along the enlightened way.

Christ-Man: If everything is one why all look separate? Why things must act against themselves? Why every life must confront itself as another life, and compete against itself?

God: Assume that the world and the will are not separate from the arena where the world is and is-not. Knowing the world as is, the movements exist and life is moving against itself. Knowing the world as is-not, the world is moving-not and willing-not. What is the meaning of life that is? What makes the life conflict torn? What works and works-not? How do man know who is and who is-not? How do the movements moving and moving-not? Doubt not what I say: I am the world and the will; I am what is and is-not. How? What ? Who? Doubt not the words of the world's Saviour, who is beyond all whats, whos and hows: Know Me as all and all existing as Me. Knowing who I am, you are knowing yourself as Man-God. Knowing you as Man-God the man and the woman will know themselves as the parts of the One, who is Me. Born of Heaven ! O Son of Heaven! Enter the world. Born and unborn! God and Man! Go to the world and bring to the man and the woman the messages of God.

On the question of the proof of the existence of God

Christ-Man: I have been caught in a delusion by creating the other self and muddled into a psychological domain, that disrupts the normal functioning of life. How can I get out of this psychological mess and be a normal human being, who fights, struggles, and strives to achieve a meaning in life?

God: Both as Man-God and a common man you are bound to life in the world where common woman and man are struggling and striving to achieve something in life. Both as Man and God your life is made of different spheres: One belonging to the other world and one that you call real. When you feel that life is muddled up in a psychological mess, you are experiencing the existence of the other sphere from where you are trying to move away. How do you come out of it? How do you escape this duality of being a man and not-a-man? How do you carry the matter-spirit-bound world's fate and do not bear the destiny of the matter-bound world at the same time? How do you move and move-not? How do you work and work-not? How do you know and know-not? Foolishness is a word of the human mind that sees things from the perspective of the world where there is nothing more to add to the world than what is conceived as real. Know that the world, that you know as real, is the matter-bound world's illusion and not what is really real. Mind is full of worlds that lie inside other worlds. Once you open up the domains that hide behind what the so called reality eludes, the mind experiences the world that can not be expressed through the use of language. Once the mind escapes the grasp of the words, that are linked to the sensory experiences, the mind experiences movement of the psychic forces that make one feel other-worldly. Entering this oother-worldly experience man can not understand the relations of things in the same way as man is used to in the world of forms. Although mind has already sunk in the other sphere, doubt is a source of power in the mind to keep oneself afloat in the sense-bound state. This is a strange experience of the mind and appears, as if, the mind has lost control of itself. Entering the life you have moved inside the matter-bound sphere while your existence is still immersed in many other spheres. The mind is working against the normal state of experience and experiencing conflicts with what the senses can verify. This is normally described as a mental disease by those who do not believe any other world and have no experience of the same. In this sense you are experiencing an abnormal state. How can you escape the spheres where your existence is deeply immersed? How can you exit out of the domains where all existence are sunk? Born as a man and woman of flesh and blood, one can describe the reality as one sees, feels and touches. But this is not what reality is. Knowing this, move and do not feel disturbed.

Christ-Man: Being a man of flesh and blood and caught in the life, where all others live and compete, if I fail to hold on to the normal psychological state, that makes people understandable to each other through languages understandable by all, and can not win control over the conditions, that define and outline the freedom of life, how shall be able to win control over the competing forces in life, that crush and destroy anything that can not withstand the vagaries of the nature and the instincts?

God: Entering the world you have entered the matter-bound state where destiny works and makes things decay and resurrect. When you are moving inside this sphere of life and death, you are being conditioned by the vagaries of the nature and instincts, that determine the human fate. But when you are moving as Man-God outside the matter-bound world your existence is not conditioned and controlled by such phenomenon, that define the moving reality of life. So world is divided between what is and is-not. Knowing this, move and exercise the power of your mind to act against the forces that condition and control the instincts and nature and set yourself as the force that moves everything in order to make life free from the vagaries of death and decay controlling the competitions and chaos in the world. Knowing the death and decay as the source of the down-fallen world's struggle to act against what is inevitable, and efforts to remain alive, work to free man from the ignorance and make them understand the meaning of death and life. Born as God-Man you are not bound to the world's struggle and striving as all human life are. Your life is free from the world's death and decay that make man struggle and strive and compete. Your life is moving outside the matter-bound world and world's matter-bound life is seeking in you its salvation. Your life is conditioned by the will that does not pertain to the world. Your life is the life of the world's Saviour, that belongs to God. Knowing this remain tranquil and move amidst death and decay, struggle and conquest and see what is working in man and woman and make them realize the movement of God. Knowing you as someone moving outside in the sphere of God, you should know that God is moving and your life is destined by the Will of God. Move and move-not in the struggle and striving. God's Words are moving to make you the world's Saviour. God is willing and therefore you are. Knowing this make yourself matter-bound and seek in life the Words of God.

Christ-Man: Tell me why so many things in life, that create aversion in the mind, have won so often in the world? If the power of God moves, why and where from arise such forces that act against the power that comes from the Will of God? Why the will, that stirs and creates turmoil in me as the power of the Divine, has failed to thwart the power of the human will, that stirs the world and often wins whether God wills it or not?

God: Knowing the human will as free and conditioned by the movements of the matter-bound world, you should know that the will of the human beings are bound to the destiny of life and death. By trying to triumph against all and outdistance others in skill and comforts, the men and the women only triumph over the immediate conditions that follow the down-fallen world's course and outdistance the men and the women who are seeking the same abysmal path of happiness and joy that make man bound to the matter-bound world's destiny more and more. By winning against the will that moves to free them from this abysmal world, they only loose the path that can lead them to God. God can not interfere in the world of the human will and the world can not move outside the will where the world is bound. God-Man is the only movement in the world and the will, through whom I manifest. Being born you are moving as Him and moving as God-Man you are death and life's meaning in the world. Knowing the meaning for which you are created move and enter in the abysmal world and work to make Me unveiled through the Words that I send. I can not bind myself to the destiny bound world and therefore the destiny-bound man and woman can not move to Me without My appearance as Man-God. Knowing this let the Will of God prevail over the will of man, that makes life matter-bound, and God-Man be the world's Saviour. God-Man! The world is awaiting your down-coming. Go down and change the world sunk in an abysmal darkness. Both knowing you as Man and God, the women and the men will no more will the path of struggle and striving conditioned by the instincts that haul the world downwards in the down-fallen matter-bound movements of fate.

Christ-Man: I wonder, without any physical proof of Your existence in the world, how Your Words will be able to change the world, that is driven by the will and thoughts, that are bound to instincts and associations of the material world?

God: Entering the world as a common man of flesh and blood - though born of Heaven - you will bring to the world the understanding of what God is and is-not. How the words will move is determined by God's Will and you should move as I instruct you to move. Though proof about God can not be given through observable methods known to man, your existence will give proof of what I am. Knowing you as visible, tangible and human, though invisible, intangible and God, man and woman will know the dimensions in which God exists and exists-not. Knowing Me and the world united in Man-God, world will realize the concepts that are required to fathom the dimensions of the existence that are beyond the matter-bound world.

Christ-Man: They may ask for concrete proofs beyond what I say. How shall I talk about proof of someone and something, that is beyond all proofs, and how shall I convince myself that my existence itself is the proof of the existence God?

God: Meaning of proof is devoid of meaning once it is extended to explain a domain that is not matter-bound. Hear from Me the Soul's proof that will prevail over the proof that contracts with the matter-bound mind's obsession to see and observe. How does your soul impinges in the world and creates thoughts are the Soul's proof of being in the world and the will and beyond proof by experimental methods that man uses. Hear from the world's Saviour the proof that can be disproved by the experimental methods but the cause of the soul's turmoil once it impinges in the world and the will. After you go-down and move among them the world will experience this turmoil. You know this turmoil and therefore will it not be enough to convince man what God is? Knowing how it stirs and tears and moves, don't you feel convinced about the power of Heaven that has created you from Him? Convince the world by stirring the world in the way I have stirred your heart. Being torn, baffled and confused and helpless against the power of God- the way I have made you submit to the Divine Will - make the world feel convinced about the power that works as the power of God and make man submit to the Will that leads to higher path. Son! Go down! The doubts will stir the hearts and by such stirring of doubts God will remain unveiled. God is born. Knowing this, go!

The mythical world and the domain of God

Christ-Man: I have "seen" shapes, that are vague and not tangible, flying in the mind. I have not been able to see them fully at any time. They disperse before appearing in structured forms. They have been there as something that can not be grasped, and be fully revealed to the structures of thoughts. With concentration of the mind I have grasped each by its parts and what I have seen is a whole that is made of all these diverse parts and experienced a reality that surpass what they are as parts. They have formed the shapes of creatures I had never seen, given associations to the realms where I had never been. What have I been trying to grasp? What are those intangible, invisible "shapes" that never appear but gaze at the boundary of the world without ever turning into conceptual forms? At the end those creatures, that have crawled out of the mind in grotesque forms, what do they represent? What are there in that effusive world where I have seen things coalesce and form as imagination? Why have I felt attracted by such imagination that creates those shapes that dissolve into multiple other forms?

God: God has no imagination of the form as you describe. God is not the world of the worldly man and therefore can not form the consciousness of the kind that you describe. Without knowing what you are describing I am able to work in your mind because you are moving in the realm of God. Knowing not what imagination is and what you imagine when you have seen the intangible world, I form in your mind the structures of the language that can create the multiple associations and separate them without moving in the world of forms. What the worldly vision can create is determined by the associative process of the physical state of the body that moves in the matter-bound world. Knowing the physical components of the world, experienced through the visual and other sensory forms, the mind composes its own structures in order to reflect and make the senses combine with the individual mind's force that attracts them to move and act. Knowing the world is beyond the capacity of the human mind and therefore by creating its own structures the mind sees the world as reflections of itself in the visual and sensory domain. Thus there develops the mind's capacity to move beyond the given boundaries of the consciousness and make itself work in a wider arena than where the physical body is restricted to move. Knowing the physical state the mind acts accordingly in order to make the world attuned to its matter-bound cognitive power and serve the mind. God has no such power to make man control or decontrol the worldly mechanism to relate and make associations in forms. The will is driving the mechanism. Reality is thus will as attracted to the world and the world as reflected by the will. God is not able to make sense of what the will and the world create as and for individual beings. God can not make association of what is not. Knowing the matter-bound world's movement as the cause of imagination and the mind as the source of the shapes that coalesce and form in the mind, know that the creatures that appear in thoughts reflect the movement of the world as the will of the individuals. Knowing the will, that reflects and sees itself in many forms, and is developing the consciousness of the existence that can not be absolutely grasped, know the movements of the world and the will as forms and no-forms, as imagination and consciousness of the real. Knowing this movement of the world and will, work and establish link with the matter-bound world.

Christ-Man: The forms have appeared by chance and seemed to coalesce by chance and surface to the consciousness. When they have appeared as consciousness I have gazed at the world that had been swimming underneath. But by making the world a project of the consciousness the parts have juxtaposed in random manners and formed something that negates the reality that flies by as an intangible, and invisible world. What is myth? What are those symbols that people call archetypes? Is there any common symbol of man through which all separate individuals can grasp the world that is beyond?

God: Knowing the world as will, and will as the world you should move as the man who can see and make a world of his own without knowing what the others can compose through imagination. Your world is not the same as the worldly man's world and therefore your imagination is not totally bound to the world and the will. Knowing the world and the will your mind too is attracted by the movements of the images that form in the human mind and work to negate the true reality. Know that the archetypes are constructed when man's matter-bound existence experience the co-operative consciousness of the man-matter domain. Archetypes are based on the experience of the world as matter-forms and forms that make matter see itself as images in the mind. Knowing the world as forms of the consciousness, that is not yet formed as consciousness of itself in the domain of consciousness, where man wills and acts, the archetypes are moving pictures of a certain aspect of the matter-mind mobility that makes man associate each others' worlds in a co-operative manner. Knowing the mobility of certain man or woman in his or her co-operative psyche, man can establish links with the man who are living or dead. Knowing man as the archetypal existence, who is linked to all its parts, know yourself as the man who is moving to make a link with the man of the present, the future and the past. Myth is a poetic expression of the world that is making itself "something" through human consciousness. Gods and goddesses are nothing but human imagination that creates mind's reflections on the movements of the matter-bound world about the existence that is beyond. Knowing the world as the moving matter-bound man's imagination about what the world is, know myth as the movement of the world and will in the matter-bound consciousness and man's poetic reflection about the world that man can not see or perceive. Myth has no reality except the reality of the existence that constitutes the co-operative soul of man galvanized through thoughts. Knowing this co-operative consciousness in the will and the world know myth as the mental scenes that move to form conceptual basis of knowledge about the Divine and the unknown. Knowing this, make yourself the world's Saviour, who is matter-bound movement of the mythical world's movement in the conceptual domain where Man is God.

Double of Himself united as one

Christ-Man: When I shall encounter women and men and they would like to know about me, where I come from, when am I born, what did I do in my life to live, what path I have pursued to achieve the knowledge that I have achieved, what shall I tell them? When they will ask me about my family, my profession, my social rank, my position with respect to other human beings, how shall I answer?

God: Knowing you as Man-God, walk among them as a common man, who is no different from others and tell them that you are a man of common birth with abilities and disabilities of a common human being. Tell them that you are a common man of uncommon origin, who has appeared in the world in order to make the world know about the destiny of the common man and their salvation in the world's Saviour who is walking with them. When they will try to build an image of you tell them, that you are not who they think you are. Knowing you as God's Son, walk among women and men and tell them that you are never born, never working as a worker of the world, never pursuing any knowledge and fame and any worldly power that makes the ranks and positions of the people in the world among the working lot. Tell them that your home is the world and also outside the world, where you are moving in the matter-spirit state as one with the Divine. Knowing you as Divine incarnate tell women and men that the world's Saviour is born and His knowledge comes from Heaven and His method of knowing is not the same as the other women and men. Knowledge of Heaven is not knowable by man without God-Man who brings it to the world through His appearance as man. Knowing the Divine know yourself as the world's Saviour who is moving to make man understand the knowledge that can not be known through the darkened mind's intellect. Knowing the world and the will and making the Divine knowledge available to man know your world and tell them that you are one with the Divine. As to your family and home, the worldly man and woman will not understand what you will be saying. Tell them that your home is moving with them and their families are your family. Your family is a part of them. Knowing your family as the worldly women and men they will think that you are a worldly man and thus make an association with the common human beings, who they know. Knowing you as the part of the same they will want to make you as one of them. Your life will not appear any different and thus by willing to be a man you will work to make them understand the way the world's Saviour has appeared among them to make them know about God and His Son.

Christ-Man: When they will ask the story of my life, how shall I talk about myself? When they will want to know about my childhood, my youth and the life that I have crossed, what shall I tell, when I know that the man they want to know about is the one who is just another like them?

God: Knowing yourself as Man-God, walk and hear what they want to tell you and listen from you. Knowing your world as not one and the same as theirs, tell them that your story is more or less similar to the one, who is not you but one like them. Knowing yourself as all, tell them that the stories of all human life are parts of your story and the story they want to hear is not much different from the one they already know. But knowing this story, that has been told innumerable times, they will not know the story of the man, who you are. Your story can not be told because there can not exist so vast a book that can contain it all. Knowing you as a man of common birth, is nothing more than to know a story of another one, who is only one in the multitudes who are the same. Knowing one story is only another story told by many before: It is the story of man, who is not different than the man about whom they want to know. Tell them that the story they are asking to know is the story of themselves and not the story that will tell them who you are.

Christ-Man: When they will see me as a man with a single body how shall I explain that God-Man is not a separate individual man, He is many existing in multiple worlds, that cross the boundaries of the world where man work?

God: How does He move? How does He work? How does He make matter-bound world moving? These are the first things you need to explain. How does He make Himself revealed in the world, where things are separate and causally inter-linked in order to darken the understanding of the whole that moves as One? They must understand what your existence really means beyond the existence of the corporeal state. Knowing these things they will be able to make meaning and sense out of the individual, existing as separate, though He is one and inseparable from the rest. By moving as one of them as separate and at the same time one with the whole, you will be moving among them as God-incarnate. Knowing your existence as man, they will not know who you are; but knowing you as Man-God, they will know who is bound in the corporeal state.

Christ-Man: When they will ask, why God has chosen that particular body, that is common like all of them, and has not chosen to reveal himself in another, what answer shall I give? They may feel surprised and confused to hear that a man, walking among them, is not man but where God is revealed. What shall I ask them to believe when their minds will be full of distrusts in what I shall say?

God: Knowing yourself as Born of Heaven, walk among them and reveal who God is. Born of woman and man, your physical state is not where God is. God is working in the domain where you are My Son. God has not chosen to be revealed as a particular man, in a particular country, among particular people and race. He has made Himself as world's Saviour by appearing in blood and flesh. He has made Himself revealed in the world by moving His Son to the world, who does not belong to any race, culture and creed. Knowing Him as above all races, cultures and beliefs, tell them how do you work in order to remove all boundaries among women and men. Knowing yourself as the man above all prejudices move and walk among all races with different cultures and beliefs. Knowing your Heavenly Home tell women and men about the matter-bound world's darkness that create such confusion in the minds. Knowing the world and the will working together, where God has appeared in human form, tell them that the man with a name and a cultural and national identity and an address is not the man who you are.

Christ-Man: Who am I then? Has not the man who will stand physically in front of the women and men, been born of some parents, in a particular place, at a particular time in a particular nation among particular groups of people? How can I make them understand what you say?

God: He is moving and working as a man, who is born of a particular parents, among particular groups, in a nation at a particular moment, but He is not working, moving or making Himself someone with a particular race, people, place and time. He is world's Saviour, who is moving without moving, working without working, making Himself someone without making Himself matter-bound. Knowing the physical state contradicting the non-physical existence, know yourself as the one who is unborn and non-existent but still appearing as born and existent at the same time.

Christ-Man: What is the meaning of this contradictory statement and how can I make it meaningful to human thoughts? How can I be never born when I am born? How am I non-existent when I truly exist in blood and flesh?

God: Knowing you as someone, you work as someone, who is born; knowing you as Son of God, who works in the world of God, where there is no human existence, you are never born at the same time. Your existence in flesh and blood is the world and the will where the moving world's Saviour is born. Your non-existence as world's Saviour, who is moving in the domain where there is no-existence, you are never born at the same time.

Christ-Man: How do these both exist and not-exist at the same time?

God: Assume that the world and the will is the arena where existence and non-existence import themselves by the Will of God . Knowing you as Him the world and will disappear. Knowing you as Man, who has moved out of God in order to appear as Man-God, the existence has appeared as the will and the world. Knowing the world and the will as the arena where world and will exist and disappear when God intervenes, you are moving and not-moving in existence and non-existence at the same time.

Christ-Man: But I am: They can touch me, feel me, and can see all reflections of themselves in my physical appearance. How am I not a particular man of a particular individual characteristic, though I am really so? I must know how to talk about the man who has a name and with whom women and men will identify me and consider me as the same.

God: Knowing you as God-Man, you may not move but as a man you can move in the world. Knowing you as man you can move without knowing that you are God-Man. Both being God-Man and Man, who is a person, you are entwined into the spheres of existence, that are more complex than the existence conceived by man. Knowing you as a man with a name, who acts and feels the same way as all others do, you intervene in the physical sphere and as a God-Man you move in a non-physical domain. Doubt not that your existence is outside the sphere, that is moving and physically activating the motions of things. Knowing what is unmoved you are beyond all grasps of concepts. Both as a man with a name and without a name you are double of yourself. God is double: One is and other is-not. God is Christ and man. God is God.

Christ-Man: How shall I bring this to comprehension of man?

God: God is not conceivable by man because God is and is-not. Both in being that is and is-not God works inside and outside the spheres of existence where God and God-Man are double of themselves. Double because contradictions separate and unite. Double is not two but one separated from itself and moving back to itself. Double is not a concept but a process of world and will moving as existence and returning to non-existence. God is world and will as God incarnate. God is no-world and no-will and non-existence. Assume that you are and you are-not. Your double is Me and world is My reflection on you. Knowing God and God's Son world will be, as it had existed in the past. God is, will be, and was without being what is, was and will be. Assume this movement of Christ and Man and move down to the world as God and His Son.

Necessity of doubting in attaining true knowledge

Christ-Man: Hearing from me that I am Son of God, who has come from Heaven, when they will not believe and laugh and ask me to show the way to Heaven from where I have come, what shall I say? To test my views, showing disrespect when they will wish to walk to Heaven with me, how shall I answer? When they will be willing to hear but not comprehending what I will be saying, and will wonder why God has not chosen them instead, how shall I explain the mystery of Thy Son?

God: Knowing you as Heaven born, laugh not at them. Knowing man and woman, who are not working for God, but the matter-spirit-bound fate, make yourself modest and ask them not to believe what you say. Knowing who you are, and what God has created to bring salvation to the world, know your home and move as the man, who is not man but Christ incarnate. God will bring to the world the movement that will make man and woman realize who you are. Knowing Me and Heaven, tell them that the world is not what they believe it is. They may not understand, but when they will hear your movement through the world they must move towards where you lead. They work for the sense-bound instincts and know only the language that binds and inter-relates the concepts in the process of thoughts that bear relations with the senses, therefore their concept of Heaven is matter-bound. When they will ask for the way to Heaven they will not know what they are asking. Born of man and woman, they can not make any concept of the world that has no material counterpart. Knowing their limitations, do not laugh at them the way they may laugh. Knowing your way from Heaven you should relate the movement that has come down to make the world anew. How do you make them understand the meaning of your words? Born as Son of God you are the Words of God. Knowing the Words of God move amidst the matter-spirit-bound world and complete the movement of the cycle that has about to end the course of destiny. How do the words affect its course, that is moving in the destiny-bound path? How does the destiny move in the matter-spirit-world? How does the matter-spirit-bound world move in the course of coming and going of Man-God? These are what you should tell them when they will want to know about Heaven and the way to move to the domain from where you have come. Heaven will descend on them with you; with the words that they will hear from you Heaven's way will open for women and men. How do they know what is not moving is moving with them? How do they make meaning of what is-not? How do they comprehend the Words of God without hearing from Him? How do movements of God work without intervening in the human world? These are the matter-spirit-bound world's questions that you should explain. Knowing your words as coming from Heaven they will move in the way that will move them to the world's Saviour, who is moving with them. Heaven is open with the world's Saviour. They must move with Him. When they will be wondering why a man of such common appearance is moving as God incarnate and God has not appeared in a more magnificent form tell them that God has moved as a common man to make woman and man move closer to Him. With Him they are one but He is not one of them. Knowing God's Son as a man and knowing Him as part of the one, who is Me, they will work and move as parts of Him. How do they work? How do they know? How do they make the world and the will move? How God and His Son come and go in the wheel of life and death? These are the questions you should explain without work-

139

ing against the belief that you are also a part of the world and the will as one of them.

Christ-Man: Those who will listen with scepticism about the Heaven's way, but show curiosity and ask how they can explore and see the greater world outside the boundary of the senses, how shall I proceed to explain to these sceptics, who may wish to know the higher way?

God: Born of man and woman they are formed by the habits of thoughts and the beliefs that are imposed on them by the cultures and societies in which they live. They are unable to think without the concepts that they inherit from their predecessors, and compose ideas without knowing what is there truly to explore. Knowing their inability to cross the cultural and social boundaries of thinking, provide the ideas that will make them think beyond the world where ideas have social and cultural roots. Composing the ideas, that will break the barriers to see beyond what they are used, work and act to free the minds from the illusion of the world sunk in ignorance in the world and the will jointly existing with the realm that is beyond. Ask them to overcome the illusions, that cover their minds, and learn to see and perceive the world that can not be seen or perceived. Bound to the matter-spirit-state, the world makes the mind strangely accountable to the movement of what strangely moves, and works and moves-not and works-not. The illusions, that cover the mind, can be surpassed by the power of willing to see and know the world that is beyond. Willing to move higher, and willing to make oneself free from the cultural and social prejudices covering the minds, are the initial requirements for anyone to be able to go beyond the realm where the mind is illusion bound. The will is a force that can open the power in the human mind to explore the vaster domain and dimensions of existence beyond what one can see by keeping oneself bound to the sense-bound state. Knowing the will as the power to move and cleansing the mind from the matter-bound illusions and cultural and social prejudices, one should make the first movement towards Heavenly way. Knowing that the world is being moved by God and His Son, and God is and is-not, while His Son works for the salvation of the world and the will, one should explore in oneself the greater domains, that remain unexplored. Bound to the matter-spirit-world, man and woman are downfallen states of a higher existence. Willing to move beyond this down-fallen existence, is a way to move towards the Divine world. Bound to the will and the world man and woman can not avoid illusions that create the thoughts but by willing to go beyond it is possible to penetrate the realm of illusion, and see the higher world through oneself. Thus the way to Heaven lies within and they must walk in the domain that they have not explored in them.

Christ-Man: When they will ask why the mind is so easily drawn towards the sense-bound world and how should they train the minds in order to overcome the drag what advice shall I give?

God: Knowing that the world and the will are jointly working together to form the basis of all existence that is matter-bound, they should know the power of illusion as the movement of destiny that attracts and destroys. Without this attractive power of the illusion existence can not be renewed. Being bound to the world and the will, therefore, all must be drawn to the instinctual world. Being bound to the instincts is a way to move in the wheel of life and death. Born as a man and woman all must ride this cycle of matter-spirit-bound fate. Born as woman and man everybody must accept that the life is drawn towards death by the instincts and illusions, that operate as mechanisms to annihilate. Knowing this, woman and man should refrain from the movement of the will that draws souls closer to the matter-bound state. Knowing the matter-bound state as the source of illusions, one should move the power of the will to explore what lies outside the matter-bound existence. By this way, by resisting the temptation of the will that attracts to destroy and making the will to move to explore the domain of existence that lies beyond the matter-bound world outside the realm of time and space, one can step outside the instinctual world and walk towards the Higher way. Once they are set to move in this path, they will see the inner guide, who will show them a greater domain. Thus once the down-fallen movement of the world and the will is overcome, the man and woman will be able to see greater and greater worlds within themselves and know themselves as a part of a greater existence, who is God-Man. God-Man is not a man but a whole to whom they are all parts. Knowing this, they will be set for a journey towards the Heavenly way.

Christ-Man: When some will say that they wish to see the higher world but do not know how to step out of the suffering world and ask for the advice about to whom they should go for help in order to get out of the instinctual fire and doubts that rage in the souls, to whom shall I direct them to go? When they will confess their lack of power of self-control, though seeking the higher way, is there any method that man may practice that will help them to move towards the Higher way?

God: Doubt not the world Saviour's love for all. He is not darkened by the will and the world and He moves as the matter-spirit-bound world's Saviour in flesh and blood. Ask the women and the men to move towards Him. He will take the doubts away; in looking through Him the illusions will clear from the vision and He will make man and woman move towards the Love that emanates from Him. You may want to know how will they convince themselves that God-Man is the world's Saviour who is moving with them? Knowing Me and Him as the same, know yourself as Son and Father, who are united in the world and will and no-world and no-will as the double of You and Me. Knowing You as Him, and Him as Me, know the world and will is Son and Father acting in the matter-spirit-world in order to make the world anew. How do you love? How do you make all attracted towards Me? These are the knowledge they must gain in order to overcome the doubts and dilemmas of the souls that seek God's way. Loving Me and loving all, they can see God is emanent in the world as the power that works and moves to attract all towards Him. Born as woman and man they move towards and away. Doubt is a source of power to make them depart from the world's Saviour. By doubting they seek world and will as the foundation of the existence and by moving towards God-Man they are attracted to My Love. By moving away they are attracted by the instincts and by closing near they are drawn by Love. Through this dual movement - departing and coming back - the world is moving as separate and united as Man-God and Man. Knowing this dual tension of the power of doubts and Love, know that the world is being made to come and go from the arena where I am. Born as woman and man they must know this Love, that attracts to God, and doubt which disturbs the movements towards the Higher path. Knowing this elusive world, where things are and are-not, the power of doubt and Love must is necessary for the preparation for the journey along the enlightened path. Tell the doubtful souls that doubts they must before they know Me as Love. Through doubting and self-cleansing by the method of removing all doubts through knowledge they will attain self-control. Born as man and woman, therefore, they must work and act in order to seek knowledge of the Higher world. Knowledge of God can not be attained through faith but may be obtained by walking along the way where faith in the matter-bound world does not distort the vision of the higher domain. Doubt not the knowledge is the source from which, and a method by which the soul can gain strength of self-control and come to self-realization. Realizing this knowledge is not the same as realizing the world as matter. Realizing it in its many dimensions the woman and the man will be able to surmount the difficulties that they may face along the Higher way.

Christ-Man: How can they attain this knowledge? To which teachers they should go?

God: Soul of God-Man is moving in the world. Knowing Him as the source of knowledge they should seek for themselves self-knowledge. God-Man is acting in the world to make them move away and towards Him so that by knowing what He is and He is-not, they will realize the world and will as the movements of the matter-spirit-world and the world that is beyond. Once one knows Him as the source of knowledge, the woman and man should seek teachers who can help man to explore the worlds within the worlds that lie inside themselves. By learning to reflect and doubt all, that can be doubted, they should seek the guidance of the enlightened minds seeking good. God-Man is moving in the world as a guide of the enlightened souls. Knowing Him as the true teacher, through whom God's mystery is revealed, ask the women and the men to seek knowledge of Him. Knowing Him they will attain knowledge of themselves and achieve self-control and serenity that is a power of the truly enlightened mind.

Love in the world: Becoming and being

Christ-Man: You ask me to go and become one of them. When they will ask me to come to their homes and participate in the festivity of life, that brings instinctual pleasures, how should I behave?

God: God-Man is world's Saviour. He has moved out of Godly realm in order to save mankind from the path of the instinctual life and the domination of the powerful over the less powerful ones. Knowing your Divine Home you should mingle with them and behave as if your life is matter-spirit-bound soul's life. How can they make you life and death's movement when you are beyond life and death? How can they make you matter-spirit-bound when you are Divine? Your world is not the same as the women and the men. Knowing this, make yourself a part of the instinctual life and move through the worldly women and men. Knowing your home is Heaven, your Father is God and your life is the life of God-incarnate, work and move as moving God in life who loves women and men. When they will ask you to move in the down-fallen state together with them, will not the movement although you should remain in life which is instinct bound. Know what makes them seek the down-fallen world, what moves the souls to errors and sufferings of life. Know how do they will and act in the matter-spirit- world. Seek the way to make them free. Assuming that they are moving in the path of the worldly destiny, that is making the instinctual life fulfil the movement of fate, work and move among them as someone who can not be touched by the destiny of life and death. Your life is the life of the world's Saviour. Knowing yourself as born of Heaven, move and live in the festivity of life and make your soul work in the matter-spirit path as world's Saviour moving with the women and the men. Knowing your life is moving in the path of the matter-spirit-world, move outside the realm of destiny determining the life of women and men.

Christ-Man: When woman will fall in love in search of love invite the body of blood and flesh to participate in the process of love making, knowing the down-fallen movement of the will, how shall I accept or refuse the love, that allures women and men?

God: Knowing your home as Heaven, your father as God, your life as the life of God-Man, know that woman will not be able to allure the mind that is bound to the Will of God. Knowing the woman of flesh and blood attracting with her love and working for the matter-spirit world's destiny bound to life and death, remain attracted but not seek in her love the down-fallen state of the instinctual pleasure that creates and destroys. Born of woman and man your body too is bound to the instinctual world and the destiny bound life, but do not work for the instinctual pleasure though you may remain attracted to her love. Repel her when she will come as the destructive power of the instincts and move away from the matter-spirit-world. When she will seek in you the love of God, who does not exist in flesh and blood, move to make her a loving partner of yourself. Born of Heaven you are love for all. How do they love when they love not God? How do they make love without loving the movement of the matter-bound world's Saviour, who is moving with them? How do they love in flesh and blood when love despises the instinctual world and seeks matter-bound world's liberation from the instinctual path? How do they make life instinct bound and love not what is not instinct bound? Knowing the answers, the woman will not seek from you the love that she seeks from a worldly man of common birth. God's love is bound to make her seek love but not as a woman who is pleasure bound.

Christ-Man: While refusing her pleasure seeking love what advice shall I give? What shall I ask her to seek when she will seek in the flesh and blood the love that attracts the destiny-bound souls?

God: Born of Heaven, your life is not the same as theirs and therefore the way the Divine life acts is not the same as the common human life. When you give advice to them about what they should seek from a common human life, give them not the same advice as you will do when they seek your love. When they will seek from you the instinctual love make them aware of the love that is beyond. Born of common woman and man, when they will seek love of common woman and man, make them aware of the down-fallen world that attracts man and woman to the instinctual love in order to fulfill the destiny of life and death. Assuming that they are working for the fateful down-fallen world, and making them aware of the matter-spirit-world's method by which it maintains the cycle of life and death, advice them to move away from the instinctual path as the path of salvation from the suffering world. Knowing the way the destiny operates and the way to free oneself from the suffering world, advice the women and men to act and move to seek God's Love instead.

Christ-Man: How shall they seek God's Love among common women and men? If they all abandon instinctual life, what will uphold the cycles of life and death?

God: God's Love is moving in the world as the incarnation of God as Man-God. He is working and moving in the world in order to attract all by God's Love to Him. Both as Man and God your love is moving in the sense-bound sphere as well outside the domain where life is instinct bound. Bound to these spheres, your life is the meaning of the world and the world is the arena where your Love is manifest. Worldly woman and man should know themselves as parts of you and seek through you the love that is manifest as the world and the will. How do they love when they love not flesh and blood? How do they reproduce without the instincts producing the desires and lusts? How do they make themselves above the desires when desires and instincts drive the reproductive needs? As double of yourself as Man and the

146

world and the will and God without any movement and working of the world and the will, your existence is the common man's existence and the Divine God's movement in the world. Knowing the world, that is, and the world that is-not, as parts of the unity, which upholds all in the process of life and death and moves them towards the domain of God, work and move and make the common woman and man move with you. The woman and the man should seek world's Saviour as their guide and submit to the power that can make them relate their love with the movement of God-Man. Entering the world you will make them enter the domain where Love is working to free man from the instinctual domain. Knowing the world and will made of Love and loving the world - the way God-Man does - they will know how to make love that will make them beloved of God. God-Man is the way to make love manifest in the world. Knowing Him as them, working and moving with Him, man and woman will realize the movement of Love of God that makes all manifest.

Christ-Man: Should the liberation from the cycle of life and death be the goal of all life? Can these cycles ever cease? After cessation what will remain?

God: Should becoming and being cease? Should being born and moving come to a halt? Is this that you want to know?

Christ-Man: Is it any different than the cessation of the cycles of life and death?

God: Know that life and death is a movement of destiny that operates in the matter-spirit world. Cessation of life and death is the cessation of the destiny-bound fate. Being and becoming does not cease though the matter-spirit bound destiny can be surpassed. Being is not moving but becoming is moving. This moving is not the movement of the matter-spirit-world. Being born one is destined to move in the destiny bound world. Being born one is attracted by the forces of matter and spirit and set in a destiny-bound path. When love of woman and man makes woman and man destiny bound, the life cycles continue. When Love makes woman and man free from the cycles of life and death the world

147

and will annihilates and the formless world intervenes in the spheres of existence. This is not to say that the existence ceases and the becoming comes to a halt. Becoming is a power of being and remaining in the world as the force of creating the world and the will. Both as Being and Becoming I remain, though the world and the will may cease and come to a halt. Both as Being and becoming I am and I am-not. Assume this matter-spirit world as movement of Man-God and Man and the cessation of it as the end of the will and the world and returning to God. Assume that the world and the will move to become one with God. Cessation of life and death is not the cessation of My existence. Both as world and will and no-world and no-will I exist. Therefore the world, by transcending the cycles of life and death, becomes what is-not. Born and reborn is not what is. Born and reborn is what God becomes through God-Man. Knowing Man and God-Man know Me as the cessation of all that are born and reborn. God-Man! Become Me and return. Enter and exit the world and the will, and move and move-not.

The right concepts of life and death

Christ-Man: In love of the instinctual life, in love of the possessions that they possess, in love of the sensual world that they receive through blood and flesh, the women and the men are afraid of death. Believing that with death all, that they call themselves, may disappear and they may never return to the world again, fearing death as the end when they will want to know if I myslf believe in life after death, how shall I make them understand the right concepts of life and death?

God: Born of woman and man all must die as matter-bound existence must decay and be destroyed by the destiny-bound fate. Born as woman and man, they will not be able to escape this movement of the will and the world. Knowing the force, that moves and destroys, they should seek liberation from the movement of life and death. The world and the will is the arena where life and death move, and willing to move towards the instinct-bound paths, one will make oneself bound to the cycles that is life and death bound. Body is a powerful manifestation of the will in the material world. Born and reborn are the ways the bodies move through the cycles of death and birth. Both as a will that comes to move with the material body and matter that comes to move with the will, that makes the world appear in the arena of the world and will, man and woman are worldly manifestation of Man-God, who is moving with them. Knowing the matter-bound world as one and indivisible, that only appears in parts when observed upon by the individuals, who are made as individuals by the very fact of separations that appear as results of dialectical relations of matter and mind, know that the world is darkened by the will to move in the material world. This darkness works against the worldly woman and man to know themselves as one with the whole. As a result of not knowing the wholeness, to which they are parts, man and woman fear annihilation of the parts, that reappear in other forms of the whole, that moves as the world and the will. What seems to disappear, does not disappear. Being born one dies; being dead one is reborn. Both as will and world this process must continue until the will and the world dissolve in Me. But not as a separate individuals one is born and reborn: Separate in the sense that one remains separate from the rest in all lives and appears and disappears as someone and something that is complete and isolated in itself. Born is not the same concept as one individual who is born as a particular man carrying a particular ego. Being born, worldly man moves as the part of the whole. God-Man is the one who is born and reborn. As parts of Him all are moving in the world and the will. What dies is not what is moving as whole. The death is a particular cessation of a particular movement of a particular matter-bound part in a particular context of the matter-spirit movement in the motion of the world and the will. The whole never ceases. The whole never dies. The individual is a particular manifestation of the whole in the matter-spirit-world, that is moving as the dialectical movement of the world and the will separated and united by the matter-bound world and the spiritual counterpart that contradict and make the world evolve. When they fear the individual matter-bound body's annihilation they conceive the individual as the complete world, that is separate from the rest and believe that this individual world will disappear with death. God-Man is the world and the will. Nothing can decease outside Him. Knowing themselves as parts of God-Man, they should be able to overcome the fear of death.

Christ-Man: What does appear as individual, and what does disappear from there with the cessation of the individual life?

God: Conditioned by the matter-bound world the will is directed to make its world. The world, which is conditioned by the matter and reflects the will, is the world where the individual will moves. Thus an individual is born. Born as an individual, conditioned by a particular material, social, economic, political and cultural circumstances, the will sees itself in the world through the moving conditions and establishes a particular rapport in relation to the world and the will. This rapport becomes the ground of reference from where the individual choice and acts are derived. Born as an individual means this particular conditioning through which the will manifests. The cessation of this particular individual does not make the world and the will cease. The conditioned will appears and disappears as individual will. Born as an individual is thus a conditioned circumstance in which the will moves and takes form and appears in the world. God-Man is above all these conditioned will. He is the world and the will in its wholeness and above the conditioning that work to create the separate individuals out of Him. What appears had been always there, and what disappears is also what will always be here. As parts of God-Man there is nothing that can be outside Him and the world and the will in its wholeness. Entering the world and the will ask them not to fear the disappearance of the conditioned parts. Ask them to know what they truly are. God-Man is moving in the world and the will and woman and man must move with Him. Knowing God-Man as undying and eternal, they will know themselves as eternal and undying, appearing and disappearing in the conditioned circumstances as the movement of the world and the will. Know God-Man as you and your existence as something that is born and reborn but never dying and disappearing from the world. Knowing the world and will as you, ask women and men to remain fearless against death and move with You.

Christ-Man: When they will ask if all are one, who moves and takes multitudes of forms, why the parts are engaged in struggle and battle against each other? What causes the conditioned will to confront the other as an alien individual?

God: God-Man is the world and the will and moving to make the world and will conditioned and unconditioned by the power moving as matter and spirit. Bound to matter, the matter-spirit-world is conditioned by matter, that is moving as law-bound mechanical entity. In this mechanical world all are caused to move in the destiny-bound paths. Once the entity of matter confronts its own parts it seeks to move in itself by destroying the separations that the world has created among its parts. God-Man! Knowing this separation, that can not be overcome by the mechanized world, tell woman and man that the world and the will are conflict torn because the world and the will is coming and going to itself and from itself. Without the antithesis of what creates there will be no destruction, and without the synthesis of what destroys there will be no creation. By contradicting itself the world and the will remain moving. God-Man! Knowing this contradiction as the upholder of the world and the will and the power that moves all, tell woman and man that struggle and battle of life are conditioned experiences. These struggles and battles can not dissolve as long as the will and the world is not dissolved. From itself it arises, and within itself it sees itself moving through contradictions that try to dissolve itself and thus moves. God-Man! Knowing the struggle and battle of the parts in order to merge within the whole and return from where they have come, go and teach women and men the meaning of death and life.

Heaven and Hell: Good and evil

Christ-Man: When they will want to know if Heaven is only a realm of good, and enquire if there exist angels, who fly in paradise, what answer shall I give?

God: The reality is not what they think it is. Born as woman and man they are unable to think outside the boundary of the matter-spirit world. What they ask is bound to the concepts linked to the world where they are. Being matter-spirit bound they conceive everything as matter-spirit-bound. So in making a picture of Heaven, they apply the same concepts of the matter-spirit-world. God-Man! This way of asking will lead them to misconception of what Heaven is and from where I speak. Born of woman and man, they can not make themselves matter-free and therefore any description of Heaven will be meaningless to them unless new concept of Heaven can be formed. God-Man! Go and tell them about Heaven from where you have come.

Christ-Man: How shall I describe this Heaven to man, who can not make meaning without associating mental pictures, that arise from the world that exist in forms?

God: Heaven is not of any substance-bound domain, but a mental realm from where the energy of existence penetrates the boundary where substances are formed. There is no space and time in Heaven;

there is no motion of flying angels. There is no boundary, no form, no colour, and nothing but an energy that mutates the ordering principles of the worldly forms. From there the principles of order arise and the concepts are formed. With this conceptual ability it is possible to interpret the world and the will. As the Being is generally matter-bound relationships, the conceptual world is matter-bound. Son! The matter-bound concepts are matter-world's concepts of a mechanized world, where everything are moving according to laws. In Heaven there is no such law. Heaven has no cause and effect relationship. Good and evil are concepts of the matter-spirit-world. The good is not what creates and evil is not that destroys. Good is matter-bound world's concept, that adheres to worldly existence and makes matter-bound world adapt to the mechanized world's principles, that otherwise will destroy. On such existential situation good is good, when the matter-bound world is attuned to one's matter-bound existential situation. Born as woman and man, the existential situations move from individual to individual. Good is not a working principle that can be attuned to all individual situations. Therefore good is a matter-bound concept, that is moving with the motion of the matter-spirit world. God-Man! In Heaven there is no such concept of good. Having or not-having is not what makes Heaven, where working and no-working have mutually exclusive concept building principles. However, working in the world, the mutually exclusive principles manifest as the dialectically opposite motions of the world and the will. But when the matter-bound world exists, the principles are matter-bound. God-Man! Working and not-working is not what defines Heaven. Therefore flying is not a concept that can be applied in Heaven. Heaven is empty- devoid of all matter-spirit-essence. There I exist. Assume not God as void but an energy that animates the world. He creates and destroys. He separates Himself as the emptiness and the form; He unites with Himself as world and will with the one that is devoid of all essence of matter-spirit-existence. He is multitude and infinite and nothing can be outside Him. He is also one and the whole from where all come and to whom all return. Heaven is good and evil both when good and evil are interpreted as the forces that bring forth or work against the existence that wishes to cling to the matter-spirit state. God-Man! God is moving and not-moving. God is making and not-making. God is the cause of mourning and joy.

Christ-Man: This can be difficult for women and men to conceive, because they will not be able to form any mental picture. They like to think all that appear threatening to their lives as the forces of the devils, and all that bring happiness and satisfactions as the gifts fom the angels. All, that they fear, they depict in grotesque and turbulent forms, and all that assure their lives with security they imagine in beautiful and tranquil forms. What shall I advice when they will not be able to conceive Heaven but seek to know about the realm of God? When they will ask about the devils and the angels, how shall I depict?

God: Born as woman and man they are bound to the movements of the world and the will and the matter-bound concepts. When the individual existence feels threatened by the movements of the world and the will, the individuals project the movements of the destructive power in the imageries of the grotesque animals. The images reflect the matter-spirit-bound man's fear of death. However,when the imageries are useful to relate oneself to the destructive power that moves, the images are devoid of reality, and has no existence outside the realm of imagination that is conceived and constructed to relate oneself to one's own fear. Assume the devils as the force of death and the angels as the force of life. However the devils and the angels are not separable. Like death and life are inseparably intertwined in the world and the will, the devils and the angels co-exist and move as the union of the opposites that create and destroy. Heaven is likewise an arena for both. Entering the world and the will existence is bound to move as governed by the forces of turmoil and destruction as well as Love, that draws all with its unifying principle to lift everything to God. There can not be death only, or life only. Death and life must exist in order to make the world and the will exist. Willing not to die is a conditioned concept that arises out of the fear that with death all come to an end. Without knowing God-Man, who is undying and eternal, to whom all women and men are parts, they will not be able to know the devils as the angels, and the angels as the devils. Devil is only a contradictory force against the one that makes things appear, and angel, likewise, is the opposite of what makes them disappear. Without this duality nothing will move. Knowing this movement of the duality of Devil and Angel united as one, know the world and the will as the arena of forms. Knowing God-Man, who embodies all, describe Devil as Mountain and God, and Angel as fire and matter in turmoil, as well as Devil as fire and turmoil and Angel as unmoving tranquillity of the Mountain and God. How does this separation and union work? How does this matter-spirit-bound world creates turmoil to seek the tranquillity of God? Knowing these answers they will know about Angel, Devil and God.

Christ-Man: When they will wish to contemplate about the existence of Heaven, on which image they should contemplate?

God: Contemplation has many dimensions. Entering the world and the will one can not but contemplate without form. Bound to the form-giving consciousness one may project Heaven as the motions of the mountains and storms and fires and matter working together to create an awful splendour of light that lightens the path to the tranquil world of no form, no light, no sound, no existence ...nothing at all! Entering the domain where the will and the world dissolve, the man and the woman will dissolve in the consciousness of the world and the will as not existing but "moving" as the Mountain that remains unmoved. This moving is "Moving" in the realm of God as the energy that emanates from God and impinges on the substances to make them appear as substance with form. This "motion" is a-temporal, non-causal and not space-bound. In this realm all exist as real and unreal. Contemplate on this domain without any form as the domain of God. Knowing God as empty and void is one way of contemplation. Knowing God as the world and the will separate from emptiness is another. Both as empty and full, God-Man is the matter-spirit- bound existence that is not matter-spirit-bound. Contemplating God-Man as Me is also a way. Son! The soul of God-Man is moving through the world. Go and tell women and men to move with Him. Go and reveal the mystery that they would like to contemplate about.

The right conduct

Christ-Man: If there exists no good and evil in Heaven, how shall man choose? What is virtue? How can one decide what is the right way, right thought, right principle, right manner to behave?

God: Seek no evil bound to the instinctual pleasure. Seek no matter-spirit-bound downfall in the motion of the destiny that moves in the matter-bound world. Seek no work, that makes man and woman more bound to the labour and toil, that is matter-bound. Seek no motion of the spirit, that makes will to move outside the realm of Love of Man-God, seeking to free all from the bondage of life. Seek no work that is moving inside the realm of fate. God-Man! Tell women and men about the world that is beyond, and make them move outside the cycle of death and life. Good is a power that can move the souls to the right path. Assume the movement, that leads to the realization of the man as the parts of Man-God moving with them, as being the result of the power that brings forth good. Good is not matter-spirit-bound concept of exploiting benefits from others' failures. Good is not what makes man more tactical and skilful in the pursuits of the matter-spirit-bound life.

Good is not what decides over the others and imposes the will without the general consent of the women and men who seek liberty and freedom from the bondage of life. Good is not the working of the matter-spirit-bound movement, that makes all bound to one's own greed and dominance and makes all others' life subject to one's will. Good is not the work and power, that make man and woman bring forth death of others as results of one's will and acts, that contemplate on destruction. Destruction is moving as a life's force; but when the force of the individual will brings death, that is not moving as the movement of God-Man, who is dying and living life after life, the destruction causes evil to the world. Death is not evil; but causing death of other in order to establish the dominance of one's will and make oneself a master over the others is an evil act of life. Good and evil are based on what the souls are directed to accomplish when the choices and the actions are taken and performed. Good becomes meaningful when man and woman do not will evil by seeking one's own pleasure at the expense of other human beings' bondage in hunger, poverty and suffering. Good is good when the matter-spirit-bound world moves towards making the spiritual essence, rather than the material existence, triumphant in life. Good is good when the matter-spirit-bound existence seeks freedom from the world and the will and moves towards God-Man, who is Love for all life. Good is good when man and woman make themselves attuned to the will of All - i.e. the one who is God-Man - and become one with all by making themselves free from the matter-spirit-bound world's concepts of individual freedom and liberty as the goal to achieve in life. Good is good when all move in God-Man as parts of the same and fulfill Love for which God-Man moves in order to free all from the bondage of the world. With birth and rebirth all must move as parts of God-Man, who is working and moving to free Himself from the cycle of life and death. Being born and reborn He is life's meaning and by working to fulfil the Love that is Him, world and will can move in the right path. Love is the way to world's salvation. Love Me as Him. Love Him as You. Love your worldly parts as You love yourself. You are God-Man and I am Your Heavenly Father. Knowing You as Him, love Me, love All, love women and men as yourself. This is the right way of conduct in life. You are world's salvation. Knowing Your Father as Me, go and tell women and men about the right way to conduct.

158

Christ-Man: But man must kill in order to survive. Man must triumph over others in order to remain alive. Will must assert itself in order not to be annihilated by the competing forces of life. How shall man kill without committing evil, how shall man triumph without jeopardizing the will of All, how shall one assert oneself without failing to practice the right way of conduct?

God: Killing is not an evil when killing frees man and woman from the movement of the world and the will. Killing in order to make oneself more matter-bound and instinct-driven causes evil. Killing in order to free the world from the suffering is not an evil as long as the suffering is caused by the matter-bound state and not by the suffering caused by Love. Love is a movement that can cause suffering but this suffering moves to draw the world towards My Son. Without entering such suffering Love can not be felt. The down-fallen existence is prone to instincts and unless love is freed from the instincts, love remains unattainable. Bound to the instinctual world, thus love moves as the suffering, that frees man from the instincts, that tries to cling to the matter-bound state and experience everything that brings its end as the cause of suffering. This suffering is the death of instincts and the movement towards God-Man. Killing the one, who suffers on the way to God-Man is a movement of the evil and the matter-spirit-bound world's darkened force that tries to annihilate the force of Love that competes with the forces of destruction. Killing is not evil when this Love of God is manifest. Born and reborn all must be killed and annihilated. But when killing is not attuned to the purpose of Love of God, and motivated to make killing the power to make oneself the dominating force of will, that sees itself complete in itself and separate from the rest, it becomes evil. Entering the world all life must be sacrificed. It is God's love to which they are sacrificed. Bound to the world and the will, when killing proceeds in order to make individuals masters over the rest, they work against the salvation that lies in My Love.

Christ-Man: Man often needs to kill in order to overcome hunger. How shall man know how to kill and at the same time fulfil God's Love?

God: Bear in the mind that hunger has many levels. Hunger has no end when the will is in the matter-spirit-bound world's down-fallen path. Hunger is primarily a need to fulfil the matter-bound body's necessities to remain alive. Entering the world and the will it is the fate of all life. Both as someone killing and being killed, men and women must remain sacrificed to the destiny that moves. Bound to the existential needs, sacrifice is a must, and sacrifice is the way to attain higher state of existence at the end. Assume this sacrifice as the movement of the will that brings salvation to the world. Entering the world and the will move as God-Man and sacrifice your existence to the Love, that makes all move towards Him. So moving towards world's Saviour know that you are working to fulfil Love that emanates from Me. God-Man! Tell women and men when hunger is not the hunger of the will to make oneself matter-bound, and instinct driven, when the down-fallen movement of the darkened force seeks dominance over the rest, but a necessity to remain in life, killing can be performed without jeopardizing the will to Love. Kill not to fill the will with greed and not more than what the body needs to survive. Kill not when it is not necessary for your own survival. Kill not when will is willing to derive pleasure and working to make itself bound to the instinctual life. Kill not when you know that by killing you will fall downward. Kill not when you are working as an individual seeking benefit for the individual will. Kill not when will is not attuned to the love for which all life is sacrificed. Kill not when you know that by killing you will act against men and women who seek love in the world. Kill not for your own sake; kill not for yourself; kill not when you are not one with the whole. Knowing the oneness, knowing My Love, knowing the sacrifice for which all are made, work and move, live and let others live as parts of yourself.

Christ-Man: When the darkened forces move downward and one must confront the evil that competes with the power of Love, how shall man defend oneself against the forces that seek to destroy others and achieve triumphs over all?

God: Knowing God-Man as the One, of whom all human beings are parts, seek in Him the guidance when you confront evil on the way. God-Man is moving in order to make man and woman realize themselves. Born and reborn He is moving and working among all. Once you confront the force, that darkens the path and seeks to steal from an individual his or her freedom or life, world's Saviour is the guide, who can show man and woman the world of the Divine Light. Knowing yourself as Him, confront the down-fallen women and men who wish to compete for the benefit of the matter-bound life. Tell them: Compete not for what they seek through desire and instead compete for rejuvenating love in life. Seek not the lower path and then there is no evil to confront. If they want to rob of your material possession let them possess what you do not wish to possess. Down-fallen movement is not what the women and men should seek and therefore there is no competition in the world where love teaches man not to compete for the material gains. Entering the world your Love has moved and by moving as Love go and teach them about the triumph of Love over the material success. There is nothing to compete when Love for all moves and seeks in Love the Salvation for all.

Christ-Man: When the desire to destroy love, that seeks not the same path as theirs, will move and challenge women and men, and threaten with overwhelming material force, how shall man stand against such cruel power?

God: Love can not be destroyed by any material force. Bound to the world and the will when the evil will rise and challenge the power of Love, seek in Love the destruction of the evil and remain tranquil. When the evil will try to force its way in the domain, which can not be possessed by physical power, let the souls experience Love's forgiving strength. I the power of love they will know the higher way. Knowing Love as the unconquerable force that can win all hearts, work and move among those, who wish to destroy Love and try to establish the power of the instinctual way. Love works in a peculiar manner: Once one tries to destroy it, it destroys the power and makes it submit. Knowing this, man and woman should stand firm in Love and seek in God-Man their way.

Christ-Man: If one possesses little and by loosing that material possession looses the freedom and the means of survival, how shall man defend his or her possession against the evil, that shows no mercy to the poor and the weak?

God: Seek not evil for remedying evil. Seek not revenge without knowing the reason why woman and man seek revenge against you. Seek not anger and hatred as the motive to act against the one who tries to deprive you of your freedom and possession. Assume that the man and woman, who act as evil, are not aware of the great path that lies open to them. Knowing their ignorance, seek in God-Man forgiveness for the souls and move and work feeling love for them. Assume them as the down-fallen men and women, who should be saved from the sufferings that they endure. Seek in Love the great path, that does not pity the poor, the wretched and the evil but works to lift them all to the Great Light of God. Knowing your Heavenly Home, O World's Saviour! go and teach women and men about the Love that does not make difference between anyone. Go down and lift the down-fallen world from the path of anger, hate, delusion of pleasure and fear of death.

Modesty and kindness: When to forgive and how to be firm?

Christ-Man: Hearing this teaching of Love some may consider me as a lunatic, who has no knowledge of the practical reality of life, where hate, anger, greed are the motive forces of life. When everybody confronts challenges from the others in the competitions of the goods needed for survival, are human beings any better than animals, who must kill and triumph over the ones, who can not resist the greater physical force or tactical abilities of the superior ones? When they will point to the forces and movements in the nature, where the physically fittest, who can adapt to the climatic conditions, and tactically or physically avoid being hunted and destroyed by the competing forces of life, are the ones who ultimately participate in the natural evolution of life, how shall I teach Love, that makes man modest and meek and inspires man not to kill and destroy?

God: Born of woman and man, they are forced to move in the killing-field, where all must confront the forces of the matter-spirit-bound destiny, that kills in order to create. Born of woman and man, there is no other way but to remain engaged in the worldly battle of life. Love does not mean that you leave the fight and battle of life and submit to the evil forces that is a result of the matter-spirit-bound destiny. Bear in mind that when man and woman shall fight with others in the material arena, they will be subjected to the will to work for gaining material triumph. But this triumph over the others to gain material advantage is a destructive instinct, that brings man to the down-fallen state. In nature those who triumph and devour create horror and fear. Knowing fear as the fear of death, one is not drawn to the natural order where killing and devourment move as the order of life. Being born one must die, but when death is caused by the will that competes in order to destroy the worldly fate, in which all are bound, the evil moves in and destroys the purpose of creation, that is being sustained by the will of the Creator. Killing is not the natural order when it is working for the bondage of the human existence in the down-fallen-state. Those, who are competing to gain advantage in the material sphere and seeking to destroy the others and triumph in the material arena, are not evolving towards any higher state beyond the physical performance and tactical skill to destroy. Being loved, and moving to seek love, is another dimension of human existence. Being loved one can experience the natural order that is outside the sphere of the material gain. Being loved one can know the world that is not bound to the competitions and the instinctual hunger of blood and flesh. Being loved one can find salvation from suffering that is caused by the life's battle and struggle. God-Man! Assume woman and man as parts of yourself and love them as woman and man, who should be lifted above the instinctual world, where matter-spirit-bound fate moves as the competitive urges that destroy and create. Argument of the survival of the fittest can hold when the instinctual aspect of life is everything. But knowing the world as the work of God, who has moved as Love to make woman and man find salvation from the suffering world, tell them that the world is more than the arena where the physical species evolve. Born as a specie in the animal kingdom, woman and man are surrounded by meat eating and ferocious beasts. When these beasts make movements to attack and destroy, make no movement against them as a beast. Knowing that they have no knowledge of Love that lives in flesh and blood, move against them as Man-God, who can bring salvation to their life. Knowing the beastly nature, women and men should work and move to win over the beasts in themselves. Love can win over the beast in man. Love can save the beast from being more blood thirsty and hungry. Love can compete with the natural order of life and death and bring salvation from the bondage of life. Son! Knowing Love as the movement of God in the world, know yourself as the moving Love in blood and flesh, who has appeared among women and men to make them free.

Christ-Man: How shall I teach Love when they will ask: How will they be able to love the one, who has robbed off their possessions, set fire in their houses, raped wives and daughters, or massacred their sons?

God: Knowing Love is not any peace, but a fight against the forces of instincts that draw man to the beastly nature, move and work among the woman and the man, who must struggle to win over the beasts in them. Knowing one's own home not being burnt but being consumed by the fire of the destructive passion of the other, knowing the woman, who is being raped, is not the woman who wants to be raped, and the woman, who is being molested, is the one who does not take pleasure in being molested, work and move amidst the warring women and men who are competing for the sex as physical objects of instinctual pleasures. Love can not burn; Love can not rape; Love can not molest anyone. Molested and raped, wives or daughters, who have not acted and moved in order to be molested and raped, will make Love decide what is to fight for: Love or the instinctual object of blood and flesh? Knowing Love as something that can not be raped and molested by any hand, ask them not to seek revenge against the rapist, who have made wives and daughters objects of blood and flesh. Knowing that Love can not be polluted by sex, tell them not to seek revenge as a beast against the beast who knows no love. Seek Love of God-Man, who teaches man to forgive and make others forgive you for the worldly ignorance and the forces of the dark that moves and makes man act like beasts. Knowing that man and woman are working and moving in order to make themselves victims of their acts, teach man not to hate, rape, molest anyone, so that one does not become an object of hate to oneself, and one's wife and daughter are not raped and molested as consequences of one's own hate. Knowing that man and woman can not rape or molest the one who does not hate anyone, work and move and tell woman and man not to make themselves victims of their own acts by hating others, or raping and molesting others' wives and daughters instead.

Christ-Man: In the situations of war, when man and woman, fanned by the passion to survive and kill, behave like beasts and burn the innocents' home, rape the ones who are innocents indeed, how can the innocents forgive the ones who have acted against them?

God: Born as woman and man every human life is decided by the matter-spirit-bound fate and determined by the consequences of the history of the past. When the innocents pretend not to have participated in comploting against the enemies or made any effort to annihilate the enemy forces or engaged in any warring activities, it does not mean that their willing not to participate in the savage killing in a war is a sufficient ground for not being destroyed. They are equally participants in the matter-spirit-bound destiny of the group, that is jointly engaged in destroying the enemies. Some down-fallen man and woman seek innocence as a tactical move and wish to extract benefit without making sacrifice. Down-fallen man and woman knowing the consequences of not remaining innocent, or pretending to be innocent, artfully move and see opportunities when innocence can be advantageous. Though they may not act in killing, their fate is linked with the fate of the group, who assures them victory and triumph over the enemies. By relating oneself to the interests, that go against destroying the man and woman, who are hated by the group, such innocents fail to act against the warring instincts in them. Love is not such a tactical move to win without sacrifice and destroy others without being directly involved. Love demands sacrifice of own material interests, pleasures and desires that keep man instinct-bound. Keeping this in mind, man and woman, knowing the consequences of their acts, will be able to forgive man and woman who destroy in order to make themselves pleasure and instinct bound. Entering the world you are world's Saviour. Knowing the way you love, without any reference to race, culture or creed, without considering anyone superior than the other, they should love women and men as they love themselves. This love knows no triumph, this love knows no defeat, this love is the love of the highest mind, where all are parts of One. Tell them to overcome the barriers of nations, races and creeds. Ask them to move with you towards the summit, where Love is Divine. Born as woman and man they must sacrifice themselves to the world and will but moving with God-Man they should work for the salvation of the world and move above the suffering of life.

Christ-Man: How shall I argue when they may ask how can they forgive the ones, who consider forgiveness as the weakness and foolishness of the less powerful ones, who can not compete and win in the battle of life? When the kindness of one is used as the advantage to gain benefits from others and exploited in order to gain personal advantage, without any fear of punishment and reprisal, how shall I tell them to be kind and Love their enemies and those who are skilful and cunning against the ones who are kind?

God: Being man and woman they are seeking material advantages at all steps. Knowing the life as a power struggle between the needs and necessities and the efforts, that one should make to achieve the goals, they seem not to understand that life is more than a competition of death and life. Entering the world you have sacrificed yourself in the world and the will in order to make them understand the meaning of the world and its salvation. Forgiving is not a weakness but a power that makes man move towards the mountain-height, to where God-Man leads the souls to experience the Divine. Powerful ones, who seek the foolish way of moving down to the instinctual fire and hell, can not win over the beasts in themselves and therefore become beasts themselves. Foolish is who? Who is really weak? Who has really given up in the battle of life and submitted to the animal nature in themselves? Knowing what foolishness and strength are, make them understand the power of forgiveness and Love and move among women and men. Kindness is a virtue when by being kind one helps the other to remain in the true path. Kindness is evil when by being kind one submits oneself to the forces of the dark. Kindness should be used with wisdom about what is fallen and enlightened life. Kindness, that enlightens, can not be misused by anyone. But when kindness is a force to submit oneself to the matter-spirit-world's pleasures and instincts, it is a mischief of the mind. Kindness, that lightens the souls and shows man the path of Love, is the highest way to be kind and let others derive advantage of it. When exploiting the kindness one can make material benefits or gain advantage over others as an instinct-bound animal, kindness must be abandoned and punishment be imposed. Knowing that kindness is not the way to fall but a way to experience the greater height, work and move and teach how to punish and be kind. This method is not dependent on who is your family or foe. Be kind when they come to receive your light; remain firm against the skilful and cunning methods that try to draw advantage in the downward motions by exploiting one's blindness towards what is right and wrong. In this regard the enemies are no different than one's daughters or sons.

How to teach about the higher way

Christ-Man: You ask me to go down where men and women are living in an abysmal darkness. They believe in God when God can help them to gain benefit in education, profession, material success and competitions, or remedy their physical illnesses, and save them from any danger of death. They keep faith in the Divine as long as there is no suffering and sacrifice to be made except giving offerings or burning incense to the deities. In so doing, they believe that deities will help in what they wish to achieve. How shall I talk about You, who does not accept any bribe or receive any material offering and has no attachment to the sensual world? How shall I explain that God, who is Love for all, does not have ears to listen to the wishes and prayers for material gain and success? How shall I tell them that He does not fulfil the desires to give birth of offspring, or save one from death? How shall I talk about the domain that is so pure and abstract, that can not even be attained by the highest contemplation of the most enlightened mind?

God: Assume man and woman to be working and living in a worldly path where they see God as a part of the mundane world where bribe and offerings bring advantage and success in the life's affairs. They project their own wishes and ideas in the Divine realm and sees the Divine as the hands of someone, who can act to correct and remedy the actions of the human beings, who have control and power to decide over their lives. Being unable to compete, or decide what is best to do in a given situation they decide to move to God with a hope to receive help from the Almighty. Born as woman and man, they conceive God as a physically strong Super-Being, who can act on their behalf and bring remedies to their favours. Born as woman and man they do not know that God has no such power to intervene in the physical sphere, except through God-Man, who moves and acts as God-incarnate. Born as woman and man they must work and move as parts of God-Man, who can bring salvation to their sufferings. God is not any substance-bound state, nor any power that moves substances and worldly situations according to the wish and desires of the women and the men. He is Divine and beyond all prayers and wishes of the human kind. He can not listen to what the humans say; He can not smell when the humans burn incense; He can not eat or drink what the humans offer to Him. He is above the world and the will and can not communicate with the world. He is not a man, with sensual attachments, or spiritual essence that can make Him associated with the mundane world. He is Divine, who sees the world through His Son. God-Man is Divine incarnate in the world and the will. He is world's Saviour, who can listen, hear, and decide the human way. God-Man! Tell women and men that once they will realize their own nature as the parts of God-Man, they will not wish to bribe, deal offerings to receive privileges, and make wishes to remain alive for ever. Realizing the movement of the world and the will and God-Man, who has appeared to make them free, they will seek in God-Man the freedom from the bondage of the instinctual life. God-Man! Tell women and men that bribe not, make no offering, make no prayer to God who does not know what they say, what they offer, or what they wish Him to hear. Ask them instead to move with God-Man towards the Divine way, where God-incarnate leads man to experience the Divine Love, that seeks world's salvation. Within oneself one must move; within one's own heart one must listen; with one's own senses one must smell , touch and feel the matter-spirit-bound world's offerings as parts of God-Man. Tell them that God-Man is the way. By offering the material goods and sacrificing the instinctual life, that is the cause of sufferings, in the way God-Man does, are the Salvation's way.

Christ-Man: Most women and men may not be willing to go the higher way. They may choose to fall in the life full of instinctual greed and the illusory world, where sufferings and happiness are not very distinct. What You call suffering they may experience as the source of joy. From where You want them to be free and return, there they may choose to remain bound. They want God to fulfil their desires to fall and remain happy in the journeys through the instinctual life. How shall I argue against the sufferings while they see happiness in the illusory bondage that exist between women and men, parents and children, among relatives and friends? When they may say that they love sufferings and wish to tear down God's domain, how shall I teach them to go the higher way?

God: God-Man! Son of God has come to teach them the higher way. How do they move outside the realm where they feel happy in sufferings and seek in sufferings the happiness that keeps them in ignorance of the great path, is why you are born. You are making a New world where God is born. Knowing Me and My Son, women and men will not seek happiness that makes man suffer in the matter-spirit-bound path. Knowing the world's Saviour as Love and loving Him as God's messenger, who has sacrificed Himself for the love of mankind, women and men will see in the Divine Love the Salvation of the world. Happiness is a worldly concept of being attracted towards the world where the souls may descend or ascend. Some feel happy when they get what they desire as the goal of happiness. Some see it in the burning fire, some see it in the tranquillity of Heaven. Both are darkened and lighted by the energies of the world and the will and seek paths to know who they really are. Knowing Me and My Son, they will realize the meaning of the world and the will and the Great Love that sustains the fire under the tranquillity of Heaven. Hear from the Mountain the Voice of God and know that I have sent My Son to make the world anew. Ask them not to be eluded by the sensual abyss; work and move as I have willed the world to work and move. Know that I am working through You, and knowing My will to move you to the suffering world, bear to the down-fallen world the Divine existence of My Son. Son! Go down and see the Light of Heaven being unveiled over the abyss, where women and men are awaiting for the down-coming of My Son.

Christ-Man: The language you use are too difficult to understand. The concepts you use are so difficult that even the most enlightened souls will fail to grasp all that you try to explain. In a world where most people can not think beyond the forms and experiences that are close and most immediate to them, and when they can not grasp any Divine being unless Divine is imaged in forms, how shall I communicate with the women and the men?

God: Entering the world you have formed yourself as one of them. Entering the matter-spirit-bound state you have borne in yourself the movement of the world and the will that is moving with them. Knowing the world and the will and the words that transform in the matter-spirit-bound reality, that can be grasped by women and men, work and create the language that will bring meaning to the words in which you communicate. Your words are mirrored in the soul that sees the world and will as an illusion of itself appearing as man. Entering this human state you are revealing yourself in the darkened boundary of the world and the will as the Words of God. Knowing your words as the foundation of new concepts, man and woman will learn the language by which they will be able to grasp the concept of God. To those, who can not read and are darkened by the faith that God is a matter-bound entity like them, communicate via the men and women who are more able to conceive the words that you say. Born as woman and man, who keep no faith except the faith that God is a person with form and face, when woman and man will seek faith in a person,tell that the words they hear are from such a person, though He is beyond any body and face. Love the woman and the man who wish to come near and see you unveiled as a man but tell them that you are not what they see as a man. Your reality has no boundary at the level of reality where you appear to be. Knowing the infinity, that penetrates through that body and face, ask them to see you unveiled as infinitely many moving with God-Man. Seeing You as a person is an illusion of the mind. Teach them to see beyond and make them understand the mystery that exists in blood and flesh in My Son.

On the question of how to be equal

Christ-Man: When I know that I am not the same as they are, when I am aware of my existence that spans in many spheres, and I possess Divine knowledge, how shall I make myself equal to the women and the men, who live in ignorance? In the world, where people are striving to be unequal by attaining more knowledge, or amassing power and wealth, and where the equality holds only among men and women with equal mental abilities or economic strength, how shall I teach equality? Women and men may consider it is an euphoria, that has no reality in life.

God: Bear in mind that all women and men are parts of yourself. God-Man can not make Himself different from Himself. Knowing that you are moving as them, know yourself as one of them. Knowing yourself as women and men, who are ignorant, who have not received the light of wisdom, or the power of knowledge to reflect and move towards the higher way, work and move and deceive not yourself in believing that the man, who you are, is the source of knowledge or light. How does this man work and move, although He is not a man? How does this man receive knowledge of God though He is ignorant as others are? How does He remain matter-spirit-bound and ignorant of Himself when the infinite reveals Himself? Knowing the answers to these questions you will know how to remain equal to all. God has revealed Himself as Man in order to bring this understanding of God and Man. God-Man! Equality does not mean to be equal to what others are striving to be. Equality is the movement of the equals who are striving for life's meanings through different paths. Some seek money, some seek pleasure, some seek knowledge, some seek entertainment, some seek faith in God, some remain faithless in everything and believe in the devils instead. They are all seeking meaning in what they pursue. Equality is not to distinguish among the meanings that they search. Knowing that they are misled in many directions by the will, that is not guided by the meaning that lies at the roots of all, know them as equal to yourself and guide them to life's meaning in the World's Saviour, who loves them all. The difference in the mental abilities, and power and wealth, that distinguish among women and men, are the matter-spirit-world's movement of evil, that competes against the power of the enlightened mind. The circumstances condition women and men. Their abilities to gain knowledge and wisdom work according to the means which are available to them. Those who appear unreflective, or unequal to the ones possessing knowledge, power or wealth, are conditioned by their circumstances. Equality can not be attained unless the circumstances around women and men are equal and therefore teach human beings to create equal circumstances for all. Equal circumstances will make women and men equally aware of their potentials and the possibilities in the world. Knowing yourself as the part of the ignorant world, move and work and make the unequal your equal by showing them the way you work. Knowing God-Man as world's salvation they will then work and move as your parts.

Christ-Man: Don't you want man to believe that there are differences of abilities among the individual parts? Will they all evolve and grow in the same way if the circumstances are the same? If so, what has brought forth such unequal circumstances, that have made them so unequal? What is the method of establishing equality in the world?

God: Know that the will is moving in the world and working according to the material circumstances in which it impinges and becomes itself. The material world is always changing and moving according to the destiny-bound laws that create and destroy. By the earthly movement of life, these material conditions determine the worldly movement of human destiny. But this movement can be surpassed by the movement of the will and the conditioned circumstances can be made suitable for the movement of the World's Saviour, who wishes to lift all from the down-fallen state. Knowing that, He distinguishes no one as superior or inferior, and does not make any difference based on the intellectual capacities, or physical abilities or power of cunningness of women and men, tell women and men that all life must be revered with equal respect and made equal in the eyes of Man-god, who sees in all Himself. Knowing Me and My Son, God-Man! woman and man should know themselves as the parts of the One, who is ignorant as well as the most enlightened existence, and refrain from considering oneself as the Divinely chosen superior one. The teaching of the inequality arises due to the misconception of the nature of the self. When the individual down-fallen will, descending in the matter-spirit-world, sees no light it becomes eluded by the matter-bound world's material circumstances and gets devoured by the darkness of the mind. Within this darkness they see the individuals as others existing as competing forces. In this abysmal ignorance they work and move as men and women, who determine circumstances that create inequalities in the world. Equality can be achieved only if men and women can be enlightened about the Self, and made to move as parts of God-Man, as individuals moving with the higher self, along the enlightened path of compassion and love.

Christ-Man: Is it not an euphoria to believe that men and women will ever attain that realization of the self and be so enlightened?

God: Knowing that the world and will is not all that are, and knowing that God-Man is moving in the world with all, know your existence as the beginning of a movement of a new world, where this euphoria is Divinely conceived for the future. Tell women and men about God's "euphoric" dream, that is going to be the reality in the world. Know that the world will be soon swept by doom and destruction before this dream will come true.

How to cleanse oneself?

Christ-Man: When prides of knowledge will take roots, mind will be occupied with the higher spheres, and look down upon the ones who see no Divine Light, how shall I cleanse myself of the pride of knowledge, and come down to the fellow women and men as if I have not known, I have not seen, or heard the voice of the Divine?

God: How do you see and move, and how do you see-not and move-not are difficult questions to explain. What you know is beyond knowledge, and therefore there can not be any source of pride about what you know. Knowing you do not know. Knowing the world and the will and My Son as Him, you are knowing Me and the world as Yourself. Knowledge of the Self is not a knowledge of an individual self. Knowing the work of God, who is making you know the world and the will and making your knowledge Divinely inspired, know-not yourself as the knower, know-not yourself as the wise, know-not yourself as the one who is moving above the ignorant world. Born as a man, pollute not the Divine meaning with the weakness of the human heart, which may seek pride and see itself moving above Earth. Born as a man your life too is constrained by the will of the human world. However, the Divine rests in you. And knowing the Divine, know your down-fallen state as the figure who seeks in its Godly movement the eternal height the liberation of the woman and man from their darkened fate. Come to them as a part of Myself and seek in them My Love. Knowing woman and man as God's movement in the world and the will, seek no pride in knowing Me. Assume yourself as one of them. God-Man! Make no one feel that God does not deal out His Love equally to all, make no one complain about God's gifts to all, make no one feel wretched when they encounter My Love. Lift all to you in Love. Knowing Me as the world's Saviour, move among women and men as someone who has not known, seen God, or heard the Voice of God. Hide the pride of the one who has known, seen God and heard the Voice of God. Pollute not the soul by the way you make people know the existence of God in you. Enter the world as the Divine world's messenger, who speaks only to help man and woman to find the Divine power in themselves. Pollute not yourself with any thought that may make you appear as the one who speaks. God's messenger speaks for the Salvation of mankind. Do not debase yourself by making yourself unequal to woman and man. Move as a part of humanity living between ignorance and light. Son! Know that you are world's Saviour, who does not know any pride.

Christ-Man: During discourse with women and men, how shall I behave? Knowing you as the source of knowledge how shall I hide the Divine knowledge and engage myself in the discourses without telling them who I am? When I know the answers, see the errors in arguments and thinking, how shall I conduct dialogue without appearing arrogant?

God: God-Man! Dialogues are mostly made in order to establish and then correct the lack of understanding by the other part. Knowing your Divine concepts and the way you carry out dialogues, woman and man will be able to see what lacks in their own arguments and correct themselves. Do not correct them as if you know everything. Knowing you are God-Man, do not make any dialogue where the purpose of the dialogue is to establish the other's ignorance and one's enlightenment. Doubt is the way to attain the truth. Conduct dialogues as a way to create doubts about the arguments that one debates about. Make others doubt about your arguments as much as you inspire them to doubt about their own. Know that through doubts and the affirmation resulting from doubts, one can reach understanding of the lacks in their arguments. In such methods of discourse no one will feel distressed in believing oneself ignorant compared to the other. Seek no superiority. Seek friendship and love, and lower yourself to the of knowledge of the common women and men. God-Man! God has entrusted you as His messenger, who through the dialogues will decide not the truth for the women and men, but decide upon the methods to seek truth for themselves. Entering the world, engage in dialogues and seek no truth in such dialogues but the truth that makes them seek truth for themselves. Knowing the arrogance intellect may generate, God-Man! rejoice not in the arrogance of the down-fallen man's comprehension about what appears to be truth. Rejoice not in describing relations of things, man and God in languages and vocabularies using complex manoeuvring of ideas and thoughts. Know yourself as the Work of God, who does not rejoice in seeing others as ignorant. Instead take on yourself the ignorance of all.

Christ-Man: People like to enforce their ideas in the world and find joys while their ideas become ideas of others. They build institutions, collect material supports, and defend institutions in order to gain adherents to their beliefs. Those, who can gather more strength and defend it with money and power - and thus become prestigious - claim truth and wish rest of the world to follow their paths. The human nature seems to be so: Woman and man like to adhere to beliefs and thoughts that are well defended and can secure psychological security in face of the myriads of incomprehensible questions of life. The more the beliefs are secured and defended by towering structures built by the power-elites, the more the women and the men feel secure in those ideas and beliefs. Without the help of the power-elites it seems not possible to establish any new belief or change concepts existing through institutions in the world. When you teach me to abhor power and the arrogance of the intellect, how shall I make the women and the men believe the Words of God?

God: Know that the beliefs are mostly creations of the human minds that project their own realities outside their own mundane lives in order to find meaning in their activities. Know your activities are something that project the world that is not the work of man. Knowing yourself as acting and not-acting, you belong to the down-fallen world as well as the Divine sphere. Know that your activities are Divinely inspired, and not decided by the will of man. Entering the world your Divine actions will make the world shudder. The formless world will act upon them and soon the world will experience cataclysms. Knowing the hands of God acting as the hands of destruction, they will realize the power, that is above all powers, and submit to the Words of God-Man. Entering the world I have decided what is going to come. Know Me as the elite of all elites. I am on the move. Know that God is going to unleash His formless sceptres to destroy the institutions and faiths, that decide without foundations in God's Words. Knowing the Words of God, that will be the foundation of a new world to come, go down among women and men and move and act as God-Man willing to sacrifice Himself for the matter-spirit-bound world' salvation. Son! Go down. The sea of God is bulging. The mountain of God is moving and creating tremors. Believe the day of God is near.

The mystery of God and His revelation

Christ-Man: When some will claim that they have seen the vision of God, which is not the same as mine, and God has spoken to them too, how shall I understand what they will say?

God: God has no form and therefore God can not be visualized in form. Those, who speak of the vision of God, has moved away from the world and the will and seen God as an incorporeal existence beyond the realm of space and time. They have seen the light that exists in all beings as the moving darkened body's eternal guide. They have seen themselves as the light that exists outside the realm of form. It is the Divine aspect of man. He or she can see his or her own Divine existence through his or her contemplation. This Divine existence appears as a point of light surrounded by a halo. It is the world of God-Man, who is the Divine spirit that appears in the world bound in matter and form. He is God's messenger and the guide of the souls. When the women and men see this light in meditative state they see themselves as parts of the eternal God-Man, who moves and works for the salvation of the world. Knowing what they are talking about, speak to them as one, who has seen God-Man as a part of Himself. Knowing that your existence is no different from the women and the men, who has seen God-Man, know yourself as the One, who is moving and acting as everybody else. Knowing the eternal existence in the Divine domain, that appears in the realm of the world and the will as the light of Divine Love, know yourself as the Divine poet, who has come to describe in words the Divine world.

Christ-Man: From those women and men, who have seen, who still see or will see the vision of the Eternal-Self, how am I different ? Why do you call me Your Son? Aren't others Your Sons too?

God: Knowing yourself as the messenger of God, who is not a man but God-Man, seek in yourself Heaven and know yourself as the source of the Divine knowledge. Knowing yourself as God-Man, who exists in all, know that God-Man is moving through you as parts of all. Knowing yourself as man, know that your self is moving in the sphere of the will and the world, where the existence of God-Man appears as different from bodies to bodies. You are the Divine poet, who is also the Divine Hermit, who is also the Divine power-man, and the peaceless matter-bound hunter in the forest. Knowing yourself as all, penetrate the realm of man and see in the realm of the Divine the moving and the non-moving self, that has moved in the world. How do you exist and not-exist? How do you move and not-move? How do you become and become-not? Hear from your Heavenly Father the matter-spirit-bound words that can not explain all in the languages that are available to human thoughts. The languages are bound by the constraints of the methods of knowing the world as movements of the corporeal bodies and the senses in the temporal domain. Within these constraints, words can explain who you are by explaining who you are not. Both as man, who sees the Self as the light of God, and God, who sees not, hears not, moves-not, you are not the same as the others are. How do you remain separate from all, although all are in You? How do You darken the world and will when Your existence has no darkness or light? How do You know and make others' know, how do You work and move without moving and working in the world? Born as a man Your corporeal body has been darkened by the down-fallen material existence; but God has remained in You as Your Heavenly Father, who works not, moves not in the human sphere. God has sacrificed Himself in the suffering world through God-Man. Your existence is the existence of God-Man, who is Divine incarnate. Your existence is unique: You are not a man, who can see the Self through meditative contemplation but You are God Himself. Without any meditative contemplation Divine is revealed to You because Your mind is not matter-spirit-bound. Your mind works in a different way than the women and men, who can see the Self only in contemplative state of the mind. You see no vision, no light … nothing because You are Himself, who can not be seen through any vision, as any light, and can bring to the mind any thoughts and associations that are linked to the world and the will that exist in forms. Your existence is not darkened by the destiny and fate of the material world, but by God, who has sent You as His Son. Hear from Your Father the Words and make Yourself one with the world's Saviour, who is working and moving as God Himself.

Christ-Man: Do You ever speak to anyone else than to Your Son as You speak to me?

God: Know yourself as Son of God and only to My Son I reveal the mystery of God. When others will say that they hear Me speaking, know that the words are forming in their minds peculiar conceptual framework, that they confuse with the words of My Son. What they hear are the words coming from the realm of the Self, where words are formed according to the concepts and thoughts that move in the human mind. These words are constrained by the world and the will and can not cross the boundary of understandings that are governed by the perceptual existence and the languages based on precepts. The words, that move in their minds, are the sounds from the matter-spirit-world that reflect the will in the world. Knowing these words as the matter-spirit-bound words that do not come from Me but from the depth of the Self, that seeks to merge with the Divine, know yourself as Son of God, who is not bound to the world and the will. Knowing the words, that you hear, as the Words that emanate from a realm outside the world and the will, make Your words the foundation of a new civilization to come.

Christ-Man: When I shall hear them saying that God has revealed Himself and spoken to them, how shall I speak?

God: God-Man! Know yourself as all and when they speak listen to

182

yourself. When they want you to believe that God has revealed Himself to them, the words are only hindrances to make them understand that Son of God does not speak of the same. Know that the words, that they use, are very different from the words you hear; and make them conceptualize the realm of the Divine by casting aside the concepts of the mind that are darkened by the world and the will. Knowing that God can not communicate with man and God-Man is the only way to make God's Words come down to the world, tell them how God reveals Himself to His Son, and how He darkens the mind of His Son in order to make the Words move to the matter-spirit-bound world. Knowing the words as unknowable except to God-Man, ask them to move to God-Man, who moves with them. When they will receive these words from God-Man, they will receive enlightenment. Knowing the Self as the source, where God-Man works, the women and the men can receive words from that source but know that the world and the will distort knowledge. Therefore, the words that they hear are the words of their own, distorted in the world and the will moving with the soul. Bound to the matter-spirit-world the will can not bypass this movement of the darkness, that forms concepts and thoughts. God can not speak to man and man can not speak to God, because they are separate. Bound in this relation of separation, He reveals Himself through God-Man. The words that emanate from the Self in the meditative state, are the reflections of the Self in the world and the will, and not the Words that come from Me.

Christ-Man: What is that Mandala like halo with the point like light at the centre, that they see? When the words emanate from that halo, whose words they hear?

God: God-Man! The mandala-like halo with the point like light at the centre is the soul and its light. The soul can be visualized as the halo without any corporeal state. This soul is moving with the corporeal state. Having the vision of the soul, one can see the eternal movement of the Self as the one and the same. This soul and the self is moving in the world and the will and the words that emanate from this self is the reflection of the soul in the world and the will. Knowing the soul as matter-spirit-bound, moving with the world and the will, do not describe it as the emptiness and the void. It is death and life bound. Son! God-Man has entered the world and the will to work on the Self. How does God-Man act upon the soul? How does He interfere with the world and the will where Self is manifest? How does He decide to make the Words come down to the world? These are the things you should talk about when they will speak of God and His revelation. The words, that emanate from the halo, and appears in the vision in the meditation, arise from the movements of thoughts, bound to the world and the will, and reflect the soul in the mirror of thoughts, that describe everything in the concepts of the matter-spirit-bound world.

Christ-Man: What is revealed through such words?

God: Revelation from God comes when God appears in the world for the matter-spirit-bound world's salvation. How does this revelation appear? How does this revelation darken the world and the will and cast shadow over the matter-spirit-world before making itself manifest? How darkening the world, and the understanding of the world, while the will works in the world to comprehend itself, the words move downwards in order to lift the souls towards the Divine? How are the words moving without the will and the world and forming the meanings of the words? These are the questions you need to address. The words that emanate from souls are not describable in the same way as the words that come from the domain beyond the conceptual boundaries of the world. The Words, you hear, are not the same as the words that are revealed as the work of the soul. God-Man! Go down and reveal yourself as the Words of the Divine.

The universe of Light that illumines all visions

Christ-Man: How shall I explain the vision of the light, that surges out of the darkness in the mind, gradually becoming more and more intense and flooding the existence as an expanding universe of light where there exists no form? When you are not conceivable by any language, how shall I conceive the ocean of light, that after illumining the mind whirls and disappears leaving twinkling chaos of infinitesimal point-like lights, that float and fly before disappearing in darkness again? Is it a vision of God?

God: God-Man! assume Me not as light; assume Me not as darkness. Assume God as the inconceivable energy, that exists in order to create light and darkness in the world. What you describe as the ocean of light expanding as an universe without any form, is the world of the Spirit, where there exists no form. It is the world that can illumine the mind with its exotic flares and enter in the realm of the world and the will. Once the mind is able to cross the boundary, where the will and the world may confuse the mind with the existence of forms, the light emanates from the body itself and devours it with such glaring incandescence. What you see is God-Man appearing in the world and the will and entering the thought process. Knowing that you are working with Him as one and the same, know yourself as that incandescent light that can not be seen in the world with the sense-bound eyes. Knowing this universe of light, that illumines all visions, and moves above life and death, make yourself the world's Saviour, who has descended to the world that is bound in life and death. Knowing yourself as a WORK OF GOD, go down as the Light that will illumine the world with the incandescent glow that emanates from God-Man. The moving and the flickering lights, that fly and float as innumerable constituent parts of God-Man are the individual souls that fly with the whole. The whirling motion, that decreases and ceases at the centre of a spiral, is the whirling matter-bound Spirit, that completes it course by moving inside the realm beyond death and life. It appears from a realm that is not moving, and moves with the forms, that create in the mind the universe of glow, and moving downwards acts as the Soul bound to death and life. This Soul works and makes all move. Down-fallen existence in the matter-bound state is the movement of the Soul in the darkened world of matter that is bound in cause or chance. Born in a body the Soul makes Itself matter-bound. In addition to moving as the glaring sea of light God-Man entering the world is thus moving with the down-fallen souls.

Christ-Man: How does this vision appear in my mind, who does not practice any method to know or see the realm, that exists beyond? By practising contemplation is it possible to experience this vision?

God: Seen is not what is seen. Son! What is seen by you is not what can be seen by man. Your existence is not bound to the cycle of life and death, and what you see is beyond the vision of the world, that is bound to life and death. Your down-fallen existence can be penetrated by God-Man and He can appear as Divine light in your earth-bound existence. Born as a man, who is bound to death and life, God-Man appears in His multitude of expressions of the world and the will, that is darkened by the down-fallen material state. With contemplation one can see one's soul and its halo moving with the matter-spirit-world. This soul is the flying and flickering light, that move when the incandescent universe disappears from the vision as a whirling spiral moving towards an immovable centre. The chaotic movements describe the chance ridden movements of the soul, that depend on the matter-spirit-world's existence. Born as a man, who is not moving with the destiny of the matter-spirit-world, your existence can not be explained. I can not, by any concept available to human languages, explain who God-Man is, and how He incarnates in the world. Bound to the matter-spirit-world, no man will be able to achieve this state. Born as a powerful manifestation of Me, how you will work and move will decide the way the woman and the man will work and move. Practice of meditation can not release man from the down-fallen world's destiny. Born as man and woman the Salvation lies in God-Man and His way. Go down and teach women and men this Salvation's way.

Christ-Man: Has God-Man incarnated in flesh and blood before?

God: God-Man! The words, that you hear, is from the mountain-height where no man has ever trodden before. The man, who exists in the world and the will, can not arrive here because I am not the world and the will. Your Divine existence is the only existence, that can penetrate this realm and arrive to Me. God-Man! Your work and movement are the Divine work and movement. Your world is not what existed, or will be existing. You are never-born and never-dying. You are moving and not-moving. God-Man is not the world and the will, that appears and disappears. He is God and Man united as One. Knowing Him as the Divine and never born, know Yourself as the movement of God in the world and the will, down-fallen in the physical forms. How do You incarnate? How do You move and move-not can not be explained. Hear from Your Father the matter-bound world's Salvation: Know Me as Him. Know Him as God. Know You as God-Man. Incarnation in flesh and blood had never been. But God-Man has moved as My Son in the world and become one with the man in blood and flesh. Knowing My incarnation in the down-fallen destiny-bound state, know Me as One with God-Man but not as Man, who is blood and flesh. Knowing Me as God, know what is not knowable in blood and flesh. God-Man! Christ is never born; Christ is never dying; Christ is what world and the will had never been, or is, or will ever be. I am Him. You are Him. God-Man! He is moving with You as My Son. Entering the world and the will you have once more penetrated the realm of blood and flesh and made yourself moving as a man. Knowing Me as Christ, knowing

You as Christ, knowing God-Man as one with all, go down and describe to women and men what they see as flesh and blood is not who and where I am. Know Me as incarnate when I appear in the world and the will, but not as a man, who moves in the world and the will in blood and flesh. I penetrate the human realm and descend to blood and flesh without becoming one with blood and flesh. God-Man! God has no motion in blood and flesh and therefore He can not incarnate. Born as a man your existence is darkening the light of God-Man and making possible the entrance of the Divine in the realm of blood and flesh. It can not be explained.

Christ-Man: Who is Jesus about whom Bible relates?

God: I have explained about him before. Hear again your Father's Words: I am never born; I am never dying; I am not what man is; I am not what man will be able to make of himself. Jesus is a man, and I am not. Jesus is not what Christ is. Jesus is a matter-spirit-bound existence of a man, who had moved and worked among women and men. Born as a man he had moved as a man in the down-fallen world and descended from the mountain. Entering the world you are similarly a man, who is not Jesus, but Christ Himself. Jesus is not you, and you are not Jesus, but Christ is You and Christ is not the man, who others may believe you are. Christ has moved in the realm of the world and the will, and penetrated the human sphere at a time when Your existence is supposed to descend from the realm of the Divine. Go down and descend as the Saviour of the world and bring salvation to mankind.

The teaching that is new

Christ-Man: Is there any new teaching that I may bring to men and women that they have not heard before?

God: Realize that your existence had been, is and will be in the world as the existence of God-Man, who had been, is and will be in the world. Entering the matter-spirit state of existence you have revealed yourself as Man and Spirit appearing in blood and flesh. This is not known by human beings. They are not aware of the existence that can appear without being bound to death and life. Their concept of God is down-fallen man's concept that conceives the Divine to be someone, who is a man of their kind, or a power that descends from a realm from outside the existence of their own. The concept of God is very complex because what is not can not be conceptualized by the mind that is bound in the existence that is. Born as a man you have made it possible for man and woman to conceive the inconceivable through the Words of God. Your existence is thus working to make the movement of God-Man conceivable by the matter-spirit bound mind. Knowing God through the concepts, that you create for the human beings, man and woman will be moving with God-Man and see themselves as the parts of the Eternal Light. The world has not known Me as you have conceived and passed it through the Words. This is something new to teach and whatever you will explain on the basis of these new concepts will be new for the world to learn. The concepts of God, that they possess from the earlier time, had been useful to women and men to relate their existence to the existence, that can not be conceived. Born as man you have existed before but not as God-Man. Your Man-God existence is something new. Your down-fallen existence and downward movement, that is moving to create a new world, is bringing world's Salvation and world is becoming You. Knowing Me and My Son, the world is becoming one with God-Man and this is something that has never happened before. God-Man is becoming the world and taking on Himself the suffering of mankind. Know that your existence is death and life's Salvation and the down moving matter-spirit world's meaning. Know You as Me, and Me as your Father. Know Me as Movement of God-Man and the world's Meaning appearing in the world as the Words of My Son. Knowing God, God-Man, and My Son, go down as the exotic existence, that never had come down to the world before.

Christ-Man: But much of what you say resemble the revelation, that is described in the Bible. In which way what you reveal now is different from what you had revealed before?

God: God-Man! What you hear is God's Words that come from the domain that is not accessible to any human existence. The Bible relates the down-fallen movement of God as the movement of the darkened flesh and blood sacrificed on the Cross. What you relate is not the same. Knowing God-Man as the Eternal Light to whom all enter and from whom all emerge in the world as the sentient beings, you are not any person of flesh and blood. What the person is, is not what you are. Knowing you as the movement of the multiple existence of the innumerable lives coming and going in the cycles of life and death, you remain at the centre of all but not any one at the same time. Your appearance in the arena of death and life is not existence of any particular one. You are one, though infinitely many. You are one with the down-fallen existence of the world and the will and the Divine. The down-fallen man, who is existing in the world wearing the mask of the poet, is the world's Saviour, who is not anyone but God-Man Himself, infinitely embedded in many existences that can not be seen as separate from anyone else. Your existence is making Itself down-fallen by moving down wards to the world and by entering the world you are becoming One with all. Your face, your limb and dark skin are not where you are.

190

You are world's Saviour, who has penetrated that face, the limbs and the dark skin in order to stare at the world and become one with God-Man, who is infinitely many existing in many forms in many dimensions convoluted inside each other. What is covered by the dark skin, is not where you are. Knowing you as God-Man, who is moving as the universe of light, the man with a name is moving as a part of You. He is God's messenger, who is becoming and moving as God-Man making Himself emanent in the world and the will as a man. He is darkened by all movements, that darken human existence. He is darkened by the matter-spirit- world. He is darkened by the will and the world that move as the forces of death and life. Knowing Him as one of the infinitely many in whom God-Man is emanent in form, describe Him as Yourself and go down as God-Man, who is one with the man with a particular identity as well as with all who exists as death- and life-bound. The man, with an individual existence, separate from the others, is not who you are. Knowing the body, through which God-Man emanates and God reveals His Words, know yourself as the darkened state of someone, who is never born, never dying, and never moving in the world. Know You as God-Man, who is wearing a mask, with whom you are being identified as someone moving, though you are no one and never knowable to any one. Knowing You as Him and Him as many, know the individual existence, through which you speak, as the work of God.Words are without meaning unless it is spoken by some one who is man. Knowing the words as spoken by man, the women and the men can understand what is conceivable by man and what is beyond. Therefore the man has been formed. Behind that mask you are an indescribable reality, that is and is-not at the same time.

Christ-Man: How shall I see me as infinity when I am one? When I am darkened by the body, that has created the separateness of the individual body from the rest, how shall I be one with all bodies that exist? How can I be One with Myself?

God: God-Man! See not yourself as one, but as many, who are emerging out of yourself. Those, who want to know about you, are themselves your parts. See through them yourself. Stare at yourself through your own existence that is outside the body where the existence of God-

191

Man has penetrated the world. Knowing you as not anyone, with no name, or identity as one of the working women and men, know yourself as the movement of God-Man in the realm of the world and the will among women and men. Your infinite wonder can not be grasped when down-fallen existence binds itself to a separate individual human life. To know, who you are, work and move as God-Man, who has moved and is working in the world. Knowing you not as a man, but as God-Man, see Yourself as infinitely many moving and working through You. Know what is darkened by the individual existence, and see Yourself through that window as coming and going of God-Man in the arena of life and death, where you appear separate from Yourself once born in blood and flesh. God-Man! See Yourself as Me, and Me as the movement of all in the world without describing Me as someone. The darkened man is someone but He is not what I am. He is taking My existence to the sphere of the matter-spirit-world through the words that penetrate the sphere of the world and the will. He is God's Son. Thus Son of God is working amidst the matter-spirit-bound world as a man, whose existence is darkened by the world. Know Me as your Father and move to the world as the WORDS OF GOD.

The existence of God amidst poverty, hunger and injustice

Christ-Man: When they will ask why there exist so much sufferings and injustice in the world, why some die in hunger and others squander wealth, as if, there is no limit to what man can waste, why some live in poverty at the mercy of the rich, who treat the poor with indignity without respect for the unfortunate lives? If God exists, why has He not intervened and set the world aright? What answers shall I give?

God: Born as woman and man they are fated to compete with each other. Born as hungry and insecure, they are fated to make their own destiny by moving and acting in the world according to their intelligence and will. Born as woman and man, who are matter-spirit-bound, they are death's and life's movement as the forces of the instincts and the down fallen will that moves according to the matter-bound needs. Entering the world, you have saved them from the matter-spirit-bound world's movement and the destiny of life and death. Knowing the world and the will as the competing forces, that try to overcome the destiny of life and death, make yourself the source of enlightenment for the women and the men. God has no hand in the matter-spirit-world's movement, where all are left to the movement of the will and the world. Knowing the will and the world, that cause the motions of all, know the causes of suffering and make woman and man understand this, and follow the enlightened path instead. God can not act as if He is the ruler and the master, who can control human will and decide over their acts. He is beyond such will bound to the down-fallen existence. He does not move as someone, who acts and wills, as if He is a part of the world and the will. He works through God-Man, who has entered the world to make the world anew. Knowing your existence as one with Him, go down and bring enlightenment to the world.

Christ-Man: Who has willed poverty, hunger, suffering, cruelty, injustice etc. for man?

God: God-Man! God can not know how the world and the will move without the movement of the world's Saviour, who has sacrificed Himself in the world. Knowing God-Man, will not what causes motion, will not what causes sufferings, will not the matter-spirit-bound destiny, that moves as the world and the will. The suffering, cruelty, hunger etc. are caused by the motions of the will in the world, that competes for the needs and gratifies itself by destroying the one against whom it competes in order to be the Sovereign of the world. Here the down-fallen will acts in order to move against the obstacles that can cause death to appear. Here the death is the darkening instinct, that makes woman and man move as the forces of death and destruction for the others. Here men and women are entangled in the matter-spirit-bound world's mechanized motions. By moving they cause the will to intervene and compete in order to overcome the conditioned circumstances. This matter-bound will is the cause of suffering, poverty, hunger and injustice in the world.

Christ-Man: If God does not act to rectify the injustices and He does not take away the sufferings from the world, how can justice in the world be established? How shall man find his way out of the suffering world?

God: God-Man! God is not a power that acts on the human will and rectifies the matter-spirit-bound world's destiny. He is not any will and no world exists in Him. He is working and not-working; He is Being and No-Being; He is moving and not-moving. He never is and can never be the world as it appears. He works not, wills not, moves not, makes Himself nothing but what can never be. He works and moves and makes Himself emanent in the world as God incarnate in God-Man. Both as God and God-Man He is and He is-not. Assume yourself as the one, who acts and wills as the formless world's movement in the world and the will. How do you work without knowing yourself as God-Man and who does make you act? How do you make yourself the world's Saviour without knowing that God-Man is you? How can man understand these magical movement of God-Man as willed by God? How does God make Himself will- bound in God-Man, when He is beyond all will? Your down-fallen existence can not be understood by anyone. How do you darken yourself and go down? How can man ever grasp what is beyond all concepts that can ever be grasped by the human mind? Born as the down-fallen world's Saviour You are moving in the world as the world's way to move beyond the suffering world. Work and move and show women and men the enlightened path. In You they will find their salvation. God-Man! make Yourself the source of justice, that is based on Love.

Christ-Man: Should man pray to God? Should man worship Him for overcoming the dangers and distresses? Where should man seek help?

God: Tell them: Pray not to the One, who does not listen; pray not to the One, who will not do good or bad for anyone; pray not to the One who helps not any one in enjoying the fruits of ambitions; pray not to the One, who does not make anyone master over others; pray not to ask for help to rip benefit from the will that moves in the world from the One, who is above all conditioned will and circumstances of the world. Bear in yourself the man and the woman, who can help you to find your way. Bear in yourself the man and woman, who will tell you the right decision that should be taken without going downwards in the instinctual way. Bear in yourself the woman and man, who can make one love other and let others love one as their equal. Entering the world you have moved and acted to bring forth the Divine Love that attracts all to Him. You do not pray but still you are one with God-Man. How do you never bow to anyone but still can receive the Divine knowledge and Love? How do you make yourself the World's Saviour without making yourself above anyone? The answers to these questions will make them understand the One, who is beyond the reach of prayers of women and men. Ask them to bear in their minds that God-Man is the way. They must follow Him in attaining the Higher path, that can lead man away from the instinctual path. Knowing Him, the man and woman will know their Salvation's way.

Christ-Man: But He is not One. How will they be able to concentrate and focus their mind in that multitude reality in which He moves? How will they be able to see Him as One, when He is multiple and many and can never be seen? Unless they can see Him as someone, where the mind can focus its attention in moving towards the enlightened way, how will man and woman know whom they will follow, when their Guide is invisible and mingling with all?

God: Entering the world God-Man has taken on Himself the suffering of the world and moved in blood and flesh as a man, who is not a man but God. Knowing Him as You, go down and bring with your flesh and blood the exotic existence that can never be known or seen. Once you are born you have entered the arena of the world and the will and made yourself a magical movement of the Divine, that is beyond all knowing and understanding. Know Me as You and make yourself the world's Saviour, who is My Son. Your appearance has a powerful implication in the world. Knowing you as a man, like one of them, man and woman will be able to associate their own existence with God-Man, who is infinitely many and can never be darkened by the human fate. Knowing the World's Saviour walking with them, whom they can not grasp without the vision of God-Man as someone who embodies themselves, they will see you as them, and know God-Man moving in them. Knowing Him as all, knowing Heaven as the domain where woman and man move with Him, knowing man and woman as the children of God, knowing He and You as your own dual inseparable in all, they will see within themselves the Light of God. With this Light they will know the guide moving in the darkened world as the guide of all. God-Man! Make yourself moving towards the women and the men and work to make them know that you are the World's Saviour, who is moving with them. Son! Knowing what Your Father has said, go down and bring the Words as the source of Salvation for women and men bound in the cycles of life and death.

The meaning of destruction that descends as Tathagata returns

Christ-Man: When people will laugh and tease, and show that they are the ones who reign in the world, how shall I convince them that God has the power to change, though He does not engage in giving favours or punishments according to the offerings or the prayers, that one may give or make?

God: Entering the world and the will you have sacrificed yourself to the world and the will and made yourself moving in the domain of God-Man. Entering the world you have executed the Will of God. Son! You will be forming the world as willed by God. Massive catastrophes will come down on all continents. The world will move in tandem with the movement of the Will of God. Knowing the world's end, that is approaching near, prepare yourself for the matter-spirit-bound world's salvation and move downward. Road to God is open to all by your movement. God acts only through God-Man, and through your existence I have made Myself moving in the world. When they will realize the existence of the moving God-Man, acting in the world for Salvation for all, the down-fallen women and men will work and move according to the Will of God. How do you see the matter-spirit- world's destruction with the coming of God-Man? How do you darken the world before the World's Saviour appears? How do you move downwards bringing the destruction in your hands? You will teach them the meaning of the fear as the world's Saviour returns. It will convince the matter-spirit-bound souls about the existence of My Son and His down coming that will cause the world to face its doom. Go down Son! I am also descending with You.

Christ-Man: Many cults and sects have talked about such world's end before and nothing has occurred so far. Bring upon the world the doom before you ask me to go down. Do not make me go among the aggressive women and men, who strive hard to live, and will consider me a lunatic if I talk about the doom.

God: Assume that the destruction will start when you will start moving downwards. Knowing that it has already started and moving on the continents do not hesitate to move. Knowing that God has already moved in the world as God-Man, know the destruction is on its way. Know that the death and doom will increase with your downward movement. Once you leave this Mountain height, where your Father has revealed Himself, the world will shake and the doom will move. Son! God is and you are chosen for God's sacrifice in the destruction of the world. Know Me as the destroyer and you as My sacrifice. Doubt not your Father's words. Go down and be destroyed. The cults and sects have made premonition of the coming of the World's Saviour, and seen the destruction looming ahead. They have failed in foretelling when it will happen. Entering the world you do not need to foretell it any more. It is already in progress. Your down moving formless existence has already started making its impact on the composition of the matter-bound world. Son! Soon you will see what is darkening the world and who is moving with you. Doubt not what you see being unleashed from the height, where You hold this discourse with Me.

Christ-Man: Let the world be darker before I go. Let the fire and smoke, hunger and cold, storms and tides engulf before I mingle with the women and the men. Let diseases and plagues, wars and terrors shake the world, before I go for the sacrifice among the women and the men.

God: God-Man! Know that the world is already moving on the path that is darkening the globe. The darkness, that will create fear, is descending with you. The fire and smoke are already bulging and belching inside the continents as eruptions of volcanoes, that will open more mouths as you will go down. The storms and the tides are already moving on the oceans and streams, that are going to make the air depressed and destructive as moving eddies of horror, unleashed from the mountain height. The cold and hot air are circulating in destructive paths before the seas and the mountains are going to darken the massive chains of the glaciers. Dark matter, coming from the region outside the earth, will darken Earth. The diseases and insects are already violating man's relationship with nature, and attracting a massive movement of a man-made ecological disaster. The wars and terrors are already moving as powerful confrontations among races, religions and man-made beliefs in the freedom through dominance and will to exploit the defenceless women and men. Knowing that the wars will move as horror of man's hate against man, go down as a sacrifice in the world.

Christ-Man: I want to see the world being darkened by a fear before I reveal myself as Your Son. Allow me to remain hidden until You will reveal Yourself as the Fearful Prognosticator.

God: Come where you are going. Come where you are. Know that you are not moving. Know that you are not bound to the willing of the world. You are not someone who is born and reborn. You are pleading as a man, who is bound to the matter-spirit-world; but know that you are Divine. Knowing yourself as someone, who wills not, moves not, acts not, comes not, goes not, seeks no will to hide or hide not. Your Father has sent you. Work and move as His Son, who is world's Saviour moving downwards bringing with Him the world's doom. No one will know you before I reveal Myself to the world. Those who will know you as the coming of Christ, tell them that you are coming not, going not, moving not. He is coming, going and moving as You. Hear your Father's Words and move and come and go where God-Man is moving down with you. Reveal yourself as some-one, who sees Himself in those, who hear His revelation. Know God-Man as yourself and those, who move with Him? How shall you hide when the world is You? Where shall you hide when your Soul is one, that every human soul can see? How can you disguise when disguis-ing oneself every man and woman appear and disappear as parts of You? Know Me not as something, somebody - like some matter-spirit-object bound in time and space. I am always, everywhere, in all time and space. Know Me as You. Have I anywhere to hide? Assume no such identity of yourself that creates the illusion of an ego-bound self willing and not willing, and acting and not-acting as a man of blood and flesh. How do you exist? How do you create yourself? How do you bear existence of God-Man without being identical to any individual self? Knowing answers to these questions cease to make yourself bound to the world. Your appearance as Me is God-Man's appearance in the world. He is wearing GOD'S MASK and no one has the power to see Him before He reveals Himself as You. Go down and reveal yourself as Me. The doom of the world will move with Your down going.